FALLBACK
TO STEP UP

Sometimes You Have To
Sing To Yourself

DONALD "DĒP" PAIGE

NOW BEFORE YOU JUMP IN.

Don't boom yourself! Self-work can be mentally taxing when you're overloaded. This book is short! You can read this book in its entirety in one sitting, but I recommend that you read a chapter a day to thoroughly reflect on what it is saying and process whatever may come up for you. The reading experience can be done with a group or as a solo venture. Start with the introduction before moving on to the chapters in any order. Go about this journey in whatever way feels truly authentic to you and how you feel. No outside rules. No boxes. That's the first two things to remember when falling back... allowing yourself the freedom to do what you need to do for you, with regard to not hurting someone else in doing so.

Thank you for choosing to read this book. It does not matter how you came in possession of it; it was not by accident because, *"Nothing Is Happenstance!"* - DeP

FOREWORD

S ince childhood, I've been forced to live in a box of what was acceptable
to society, church and my immediate circle aka my family and friends.

Never one to completely assimilate, I combated a lot of stuff
designed to prevent my evolution from Donald to DēP. Despite being
charged to do everything in excellence, I was taught to spend more energy
coloring in the lines of acceptance and rewarded with opportunities rather
than developing my own uniqueness and my ultimate purpose(s). I continue
to reevaluate my decision to undo the hindrances that programmed behaviors
and the thought processes I've picked up from society, religion, media and
life experiences taught.

About my moniker… Daily, people are enamored or confused about why
I choose to be called DēP. Instead of accepting my request to be addressed
how I deemed accurate, a response to my need to flee insufferable
programming, most people wanted to believe it had some sexual undertone,
which couldn't have been further from my reality. Truth is, the way I was
brought up, sex was a sin; and after making a covenant with God to abstain,
it was the furthest thing from my mind. Hell was a threat and to avoid
ending up there, the balance of living and not ending up there began. How
did dubbing myself take that journey with most was foreign to me. All I
knew was that I didn't resonate with the name Donald, and it didn't feel like
it was a correct label of what my life work would be. This was partly due to
the fact that my father, whom I'm named after, was missing in action from
the age of three. Not resonating with the name "Lil Don" as an adult, I knew
I wanted to define my own story under my own mantle. I realized at a young
age that words, especially names, have meanings, and chose to redefine my
meaning starting with my name. I landed at DēP a few years later after an ex-
girlfriend started calling me Donald Eugene. I don't know where the hell she

got that from! But with me wanting to keep my given name and make it in some way a part of my chosen one, I kept my first and last initials and added the "ē" later. When researching this phonetical DēP. I found the definition of "deep" means to divulge lower than the surface level of meaning and understanding on any subject matter. That definition was me! At that time, all I knew was that I wanted to sing. I knew that I didn't want to become the approved music career role of a gospel artist and I knew I was not a preacher, at least not in the typical sense. I had no idea the depth of character and purpose my renaming would journey. My name and career change, documented by Vibe magazine, was my entrance to the R&B world where I signed my first record deal with DC's Versatile Records. I figured I was dating, had lost my virginity, had an unplanned baby scare, I could talk about all of those experiences because I was experiencing the stereotype of the Rhythm and Blues (R&B) artist. So R&B was the safer and more honest genre for me. But, my arrival to that world was not easy.

I was born in Houston, Texas into a southern family deeply steeped in the gospel music world, thanks to my mom Karen being a lifelong member of the Southeast Inspirational Choir along with other aunts, uncles and god-parents; I was also a PK aka a preacher's kid. Like most children were taught at that time, unless I was "on program" in church, I was raised to be seen and not heard. Real communication with explanation was an unknown concept, and thousands of rules blocked me from necessary childhood explorative experiences; like adults are always right; faith means no questioning for understanding or clarity; never talk back; simply do as you are told; sex outside of marriage is a sin; R&B music leads to sin and separation from the church; Halloween is for the devil; *Martin*, my favorite TV show, was too adult for me; get a college degree and the debt that comes along with it; get a "real" job, trust God and the rest would follow. To disagree or disobey meant a whooping, punishment, writing reports and more. Throughout grade school, I went to magnet schools where like many I had to audition, maintain certain grades, and navigate scholastic achievement while figuring out peer acceptance. I was a member of Outreach Missionary Baptist church in what was considered the Black side of town while growing up in a neighborhood where I was a member of one of the wo Black families on my street. Thus, I learned a game of balance and adaptation. The schools taught me the craft of my musical talents while the church instilled in me the passion of sharing and emoting it. To navigate all of this, I built a close connection with the characters of the popular comic book series, *X Men* as the personalities reminded me of my daily journey of fitting into my multiple environments. I always had a particular connection to the characters with mental powers. I was cool with the book heads/nerds, in crowd, singers, jokesters, church kids, PKs (preachers' kids), and on and on. I became an adaptive version and staple in each group. During that time, at no point did I consider myself cute let alone sexy. Though my mother dressed me and my sister who was eight years my junior well and I heard adults say that I was a "cute little boy", I didn't identify as attractive which wasn't a thing until later in high school. That was one of the first mindsets I had to work to fall back from since cute tends to be associated with certain unappealing elements I would work to dispel for years to come. Took a long for me to say aloud that I think I look good!

I've long since struggled with being in the "in crowd" and battling the misconceptions of what that means. Since I am typically the person that gets along with everyone, it was a boom when I realized everyone didn't like me; not for real and not for any specific reason. I'm one of those people who draw people to them naturally but didn't know how to balance the difference between availability and accessibility. The church calls it anointing; the labels call it the 'it-factor'; the world calls it influencer, while my ex called it flirty. Meanwhile, I was just doing me. Hear this: everybody that needs you close doesn't need to be equally close to you. I was fortunate to be raised into a family with relationship extensions that would create bonds that blood ties couldn't make any thicker. These were my first friends. They were real friends. They were family then and still are. I defined friendship and relationship based off those lifelong ones, and it was the worst thing I could do because... everyone doesn't mean you well, most times unintentionally so, even if they come in with smiling faces and good intentions. I was looking to recreate relationships against near impossible definitions. I found myself the scapegoat in situations and deemed guilty before I even knew what was going on. Freedom came when I learned how to identify the things that I was guilty of. I do believe that thought we cannot control people's perceptions, we are responsible for the experience we provide when interacting with others. As I got older, accomplished more and became more aware of myself and my purpose, I was perceived as know-it-all, "Hollywood", considered a threat by insecure leaders in the same circle, and so much more. Fortified by a stern demand for excellence from my mother and some prominent mentors in my life, I was instilled with the quest for knowledge through reading, practice, organization, attention to detail, hard work, music, speech, cleanliness, dressing well, respecting women and "not giving God No Junk!", which all when combined with my inner Virgo, made me a force to be reckoned with. Unfortunately, those traits did not translate to being cool or defined a "straight black man" in the early 1980's. Not in a "ha-ha" kind of way, but it's funny how all the traits that it takes to be a leader were feminized and removed from the description of masculinity in the Black culture. I often ponder that perhaps that's the reason we always HAVE to go back to Martin, Malcolm and so on to reference Black male leaders that the majority recognize as such. Talk about systemic…

OK, back to my childhood. With me being considered "cute", funny and possessing in front of camera talents, I learned a unique balance of how to act the part of the cool guy who everyone gets along with by shrinking and minimizing in environments where my talents, input and skillsets were perceived a threat and still honing those gifts and going all in when I had an opportunity to showcase them. My Aunt Linda would call me a "ham" in those moments, lol. A term used by some southerners to describe a person who sucks up the attention in a room. By high school, I was in advanced placement (AP) classes with one group; skipping class to attend all of the lunches with another; and clicked up with an entirely different group in the Gospel Choir of Westbury where I landed after leaving Houston's High School for Performing and Visual Arts. While becoming cool with the cheerleaders and some of the athletes because of performances at pep rallies, it's safe to say that I was marginally popular for one reason or another. It is crazy now to think that being in the "in crowd" made me believe I had to shrink to maintain my membership when all the while I was never created to really fit in it. I had to ask myself, "Where did that thinking come from?" I traced it back to my childhood upbringing. That seed was planted then. I dealt with that all the way into adulthood and even as recent as being a member of Kanye West' Sunday Service Collective. Groupthink, FOMO, and the desire to be accepted can be very toxic. I recall a memory from visiting gospel pioneer, the late great Brenda Waters, at a hospital with my mom. She said, 'Paige, you shole can sing and that's good cause I was worried about you, I wasn't too sho.' With a lowered head and half smile, I replied, "Oh, God is good, I'm just trying to do what I can", I had been trained to show humility ever since I could remember when someone gave me compliments about my singing and piano playing. She said, 'Now stop! This is our fault we taught y'all that and that ain't right. What do you think God is thinking when someone gives you a compliment about a gift that he gave you and you can't even say thank you. Can you sing? Did God give you a gift? Say thank you and keep going. Ain't nothing wrong with that! You must be able to receive a compliment.' She made me walk out of that hospital room, reenter and start all over again. That moment changed my life, though it would take years for me to fully walk in the understanding that being humble wasn't defined by minimization nor did it give me an auto-pass to salvation, heaven or make others think I was "good".

It took a while for me to realize that I had started to shrink in almost every aspect of my life in order to be accepted, non-confrontational, escape the stereotypes of being "Hollywood", dispel the myths of my unexplored sexuality and so much more that I dare not attempt at touching at this time. I had learned how to do so without it being perceived as such. However, self-minimization became the thing I had to work the hardest to get rid of. At the age of 17, when my abusive stepfather kicked me out of my childhood home, I was not ready to be a man on my own and deal with the realities of the world. However, I could always get my books from a bad hand dealt. Come meet me at a Spades table and see lol. I realize now that though I was a child performer with what in many other ways was a great support system, I learned to shrink because anything less meant that I was arrogant, prideful and destined to hell. What a way to start the journey of a leader and entrepreneur. I could go on about the highs and lows of my childhood, but I figure that can be shared at another time in another book... Rebirth. That journey will take you through a world filled with laughs, deceptions, joy, pain, hurt, fear, loss, beatings, success, more loss, sexuality, fatherhood, corruption, mess, drama, lies, forgiveness, healing and everything in between... that book cometh lol. I need you to know that "life for me ain't been no crystal stair"- L. Hughes, but I walked those raggedy ass little stairs I'd been given and climbed them from one level to the next from Houston to Tyler and right on to DC... Let's just say that none of those childhood trainings, experiences or thoughts prepared me for the world of R&B and I would have to learn smack dab in the midst of it.

Upon entering R&B, I was told I was too wordy which was not urban enough and that I had abs, therefore I was "sexy". Since sex sells, shut up, sing, show skin, and only talk/sing about sex. That needed to be my focus and thus the sexier version of me was born and has held a strong presence in my life ever since although It took forever for me to subscribe to the idea of it. Hell, as far as I and my super thick cousins was concerned, I was not sexy, I was just skinny. I was told that my songs and interview topics should be limited to sex, begging or I'm sorry. You can't imagine how limiting that was, and how it ultimately began the slow death of my creative freedom. You wouldn't believe the number of hours I've spent trying to accomplish a process of being commercial by standards of my community and the "machine". Ironically, I learned how to give that artistic training, performance excellence, commercial selling and it factor to others, but couldn't give it to myself. Would you believe that I killed DēP's purpose before it even got off the ground. I allowed it to be redefined by limiting terms which was a contradiction of the whole point. I can hear My Mida now saying, "the whole point" lol. Funny how we can allow our purpose to be killed in order to be "successful" and ultimately miss out on a full life experience. Since then, I've performed around the country and abroad as a solo recording artist and a supporting vocalist to greats such as Beyonce, Kanye West, John Legend, Bruce Springsteen and more. I have mentored, trained, contracted and worked with some of the dopest talent this world has ever seen including several newcomers such as recording artist Teamarrr. I have helped raise a son who has the guts early on that I never had and has since become my biggest fan and biggest trigger simultaneously. I have acted and modeled in too many commercials, magazines, tv-shows, movies and stage performances to name. I have become a thought provocateur, creative director, vocal arranger, an owner of several business and a confident leader who also knows how to fallback and follow, if it makes sense and respect is present!

I realized quickly that pain may be a factor, but not a deterrent from giving my all. I started escaping those walls of bondage a few years ago but it wasn't until the COVID 19 pandemic and subsequent lockdown that I really entered that mindset completely and have been walking in purpose ever since. Through meditation, isolation, God, SELF, focus and watching certain Netflix documentaries that depicted the life of various dreamers, the fire of individuality within me was reignited. One of the ironies of life is that you can have success while missing out on the big reward. It hasn't been an easy road as the journey through self-work and purposeful arrival can be a strenuous one. Give yourself grace. Conversely, I have been fortunate to have some really great examples of friends, family, fans and loved ones who have supported me for years, and for them I am grateful. One of my mentors, author Marione Brooks, educated me on a term called the wounded bird syndrome which applied to me and became the most recent thing I've had to fallback from. The wounded bird syndrome is the subconscious desire to spend more time, resources, energy and connection with those that I realize need me all in an attempt to fix them; even when they haven't asked. That is a necessary element when working with and doing life with other people, but it leaves you at a disadvantage when it comes to reciprocity, refueling, and expecting what you give back. You can be seasonally good for someone, and never get a return from them in that same capacity. It happens by placing people in positions not meant for them. Under that mindset, I've gained and lost a few big miscategorized friends, a relationship with someone I truly love, and had the foundation of my comfort zones shook which was all necessary.

Thanks y'all (shrug). Crazy how it's common for people to play a huge role in the demise of someone or something great. Question, why are we so passionate for acceptance from the people who are swift to end us? Answer, mostly because people tend to play a major role in our successes and growth lessons. Filing people accordingly is the best way to avoid isolation while authentically engaging without self-compromise. I had to intentionally reconnect and build new relationships with members of my village that I found in all walks of life to balance my desire to connect and help heal others who are not. These healthy relationships are mutually beneficial.

At year cycle 38, I made a vow to give my all in everything I do without minimizing or apologizing for the favor, gifts, it-factor and presence I possess. I choose excellence even if it doesn't look like the popular definition of today's standard. Truth be told, I don't even fit the bill of those my ethnic community currently chooses to elevate... never have. Grateful, as legends never really do. DēP, I choose you... again.

TRANSPARENCY
DISCLAIMER

I am not a doctor or medical professional. I have a gift that has always made me the "go to" for so many for advice on many life topics. Through my experiences and education in entertainment, teaching, communication, counseling, relationship liaison, business ownership and operator, community health work, public speaking, empowerment, human connectivity, and an uncanny ability to be truly neutral, I have helped people successfully navigate some of life's toughest transitions. Those transitions have included personal development, business consulting and growing, dating, entrepreneurship, divorce, overcoming fear, managing mental health, addiction, breaking down personal strongholds and more. The combination of all of that and my program coordination training and experiences resulted in me creating The DēP Experience, tailor-made interactions designed to commemorate, heal, build and inspire those who are a part of the moment.

I originally began personal and business consulting in 2010 and provided this service to friends, family, and my entertainment business clientele. Even while doing all of that, self-work didn't stop! I evolved from being a go-to singer and performer to someone that brands and creatives seek out for development. It was during this metamorphous that I added another chapter to my book of passions. When consulting, I've found there is always an entrenched idea or something that prevents a person or a brand's ability to achieve a goal. Some call it trauma, I call it living. In every case, there was something, a mindset or someone, the person or entity needed to fallback from for them to step up to a higher level.

This book highlights 30 of the most common trends I've frequently encountered while helping others navigate their journey. It takes a constant awareness to not return to old habits since they do die hard, even when we know they are killing us. I dedicate this book to everyone doing the work to becoming the best versions of themself.

To the building of **YOU = Your Own Universe.** I have survived and you can too. You see, I couldn't become a victim of my circumstances, and allow those reasons why to eclipse my reason to forgive myself. To forgive others. To heal. To move on. To learn from. To teach. To grow. To Fallback and To Step Up!

TABLE OF CONTENTS

INTRODUCTION

Fallback: To abandon, leave behind, remove, replace, categorize, do less of, give less to

Step Up: To accomplish, arrive, win, grow, achieve, gain, launch, receive more; ascend.

Recognize, reach and use your full potential to achieve your true purpose by living in a completely free manner; a state of living developed from the inner and outside influences and experiences of comfort; decide to apply. Your purpose has less to do with how others see you and more to do with how you see yourself. If you are not operating in truth, you are dampening your own personal superpower. Many of the most highly decorated and celebrated people in history dared to live life their way. They were ridiculed before they were ever celebrated… several, even in death, are still judged without the ability to defend themselves. Accepting that, you realize just how moot proving your point, gaining closure, or being right is. People see you how they want to. Their vision doesn't determine your purpose's impact. You are exactly where you are based off the decisions you have or have not made.

Living in truth will recourse the trajectory of your life to an upward momentum and land you on the level where you were created to reside. In other words, truth will get you to your purpose. Live in truth by understanding your strengths and weakness; taking ownership of where you are in life; and being honest with yourself about the good, the bad and the ugly of who you are. Those things you don't like about yourself, work on them as opposed to ignoring or making excuses for them. You can start and restart living in truth at any time, and as many times as you need to create good habits. That restart is a new phase, absent of the progress-stifling things that may have happened before so don't get stuck! Get over the past and the attention-distracting "what had happened-isms" The quality of your future depends on your ability to move on. Life is full of lessons as nothing is happenstance. The purpose of a lesson is to prepare you for a higher level with bigger payouts. If you find yourself stuck on a certain level, seek out the lesson and learn it. Once you have learned the lesson, expect to be tested on it. The arrival of the test shouldn't surprise you. It is necessary to ensure you have mastered that lesson. When you pass it, you will be on your way to the next level, lesson and a new test. Once you've passed a test, it's no longer a test but simply a refresher course on a mastered subject.

Are you ready to step up? Get uncomfortable… Growth is painful, but some pain can hurt so good!

Chapter 1

FALLBACK FROM UNNECESSARY MUST-HAVES

There are some things we unconsciously allow to consume our resources, time and energy; things we consider must-haves based on routine, what we want or what we are used to having. If you can live without it, these things fall under the category of unnecessary must-haves. These things can range from a cigarette to a relationship and are things that waste your most valuable currency, your time. Be real with yourself and take a poll on your spending habits: social outlets, eating, attention-seeking actions, social media engagement, entertainment intake and overall living habits. What things do you find unnecessary? These things are your personal unnecessary must-haves. Now take another poll of the things you have wanted to get or experience, but have not been able to accomplish because of time, finances or poor planning. Transfer the energy and resources that you are using on the unnecessary must-haves to accomplish the things on your "want" list and begin to achieve everything you can imagine and beyond.

Tips & Thoughts:

- Skip five monthly happy-hour hangouts and use that money to book an international flight to a destination of your dreams. You can have happy hour there.

- Replace social media time with doing something productive for your own business goals. Invest in a website, stock or a business plan as opposed to an outfit.

- Why purchase another pair of shoes to wear on a red carpet laid out to celebrate someone else's accomplishment? There's no issue with celebrating someone else, but this is one of the areas you should reevaluate as I did. I work primarily in the entertainment industry. Although imaging and socializing play a part in the need for entertainment visibility, I had to realize just how much money I was spending on attending events just to be in the scene. I spent a lot of money on wardrobe, travel, drinks, and more. And, when it was time to pay for my own publicist, events, or projects, I didn't have the resources and was looking for the hookup. But at least I get the likes and people think I'm "on" right? Wrong! We waste so many resources on perception and commit very little to the actual work.

MOVING ON...

We all have things or people that have become an unnecessary part of our life's routine. Being with them has become so second nature that we don't even realize we've become dependent on their presence without any return on the investment of time. Recognizing that puts us in a perfect position to determine if they are necessary. Even that cup of must-have coffee, relaxing cocktail, hit of "cigaweed" or that addictive companionship loses value when it begins to compromise true must-haves like our good health. Im not saying go cold turkey but are you balancing? BALANCE IS KEY. Anything that is not a must-have can be replaced and brought back if the time ever becomes right. Don't get stagnant. Rotate those unnecessary must-haves to achieve your goals. You need the energy and resources the removal of them will provide.

TRY THIS:

Map out your daily routine by taking notes on everything thing you do and every place you go for one week. Take inventory on the things you spend your time, energy and money on and see what was necessary to survive on. The following week, remove a couple of them and document any energetic or financial savings. Do this weekly until you've found them; the unnecessary must haves.

Now utilize the available resources to accomplish something on your to do or desire list. Unnecessary must haves don't have to be removed permanently. However, if you are trying to accomplish things that seem to be unattainable, the temporary replacement of them can become the seed of your achievement. You will either realize that you no longer want them or find out ways to have them without the compromise of any future goals or the realization of specific wants.

Chapter 2

FALLBACK FROM PLACING YOURSELF LAST AND EXPECTING OTHERS TO PUT YOU FIRST

Your golden rule should be "do unto yourself as you want others to do unto you". You are your own prototype. It isn't anyone else's job to do better by you. People take their cues on how to treat you based on how you treat yourself. Stop loving on others better than the way you love on yourself. This applies to friendships, relationships, and any other "situationship" you find yourself in. I had someone tell me it was hard being my friend once I stopped putting them first. Truth is, they were absolutely right. The way that I had operated in our friendship as some unofficial life guide did make friendship hard with me, for them; no matter what my intentions were. When I realized and changed my role, the friendship suffered because I never set those standards as an initial requirement. I created a dependency that wasn't healthy for us. I had forgotten my own positioning This revelation of my devaluing resonated as I evaluated scenario after scenario, and realized I was responsible for the development and ultimate destruction of it. Ironically, this scenario played out during my birthday season and I had to accept if I couldn't recenter and put myself first during that time, it would never be my time.

People will try you if they think they can get away with it. This is the reason people interact with certain people differently than they act with you. They tease and make fun of one person while respecting and praising another. How people treat you is a direct reflection on how they see you. You give them what they see. I've been told I am "bougie" because of my preferences by people that don't share my experiences and interests in the same. Instead of accepting my preferences, they chose to internalize how my selections made them feel and consequently deflect. People often attach derogatory labels like this when it's contrary to the decisions they make for themselves. While they opt to eat a dollar burger daily, I opt to set a budget to eat where I want, when I want; like my favorite Hawaiian rib-eye steak every other week. I don't judge anyone for doing so as there are times that I cook and eat in to achieve specific goals. But for a time, I allowed that judgmental descriptor of who I am to offend me because it wasn't delivered as a compliment. Later I understood being called "bougie" was that person's way of saying I chose something they consider better than their own choice. This expression of their less-than feeling was nothing for me to internalize. The thing is, I do what I like for me, and make certain sacrifices for it. Staying true to that has made others acquiesce to that standard when including me in their plans or doing something for/with me. And that's good. Show others how to treat you by letting them see you do it for yourself. If you don't set what is mandatory consideration and treatment for yourself, how will they know what it is?

We all make decisions and have preferences. Get okay with someone having theirs. True to the dark and judgmental side of human nature, many people deflect their feelings of inferiority when comparing their preferences or acquisitions to another's. They do this without even realizing it. They attack others with statements such as, "you think you are all of that", or my personal favorite, "you are so Hollywood, superstar". Don't own that shit! Though it can be offensive, replace offense with celebration. Celebrate the fact that you are being authentic to yourself and the placement you deserve. Though they judge, they recognize where you are. Secretly, they admire it, and it's why they long to stick around. You'll get that same "wyd" text from them every weekend. The same people who call me "bougie" only give or invite me to the best experiences. I win. You don't have to shrink to accommodate someone else's ego. They will either step up or crouch down to help you step up. Learn to position people accordingly as people are in your life for a reason, season or lifetime. Everybody shouldn't be assessed or handled the same. I no longer give the time and access to those that truly can't take me doing me. Unfortunately, common courtesy isn't common at all, but respect of self-worth can be. Even when you don't recognize your projection of your own value, others see it. You are your number one priority and frankly, no one can love you better than you can love yourself. You can however get them pretty damn-close through example. First place is never given, it is taken! In what position are you placing yourself?

TRY THIS:

Think about your circle and ask yourself who truly supports and accepts you as you are. When constructive criticism is given, and friends should be able to do this, what is the motive? Is their input supported? What is their intent? Now weigh how you show up for them. Do you feel they ever show up for you? You don't have to cut people off necessarily, but you should strategically place them where they need to be. Tenure, routine and convenience should not be the sole determining factors for how much access you give someone. As you grow and evolve, remember that everybody can't get in the boat.

Chapter 3

FALLBACK FROM NEEDING ACCEPTANCE

You are enough and many people won't accept that. Once you've reached a certain level of success, some will begin to give you public accolades just to be associated. Others will say that you aren't enough just because they can't handle your popularity. Conversely, a small group of people will publically appreciate you and what you have to offer without expecting a return. This just means you can never do enough to get people's full acceptance, and if that's what you are living for, then you have set an unreachable goal. That revelation has been devastating for many and in some cases, detrimental. Learn it now! Most people are successful because they operate in their purpose outside of the need for anyone else to affirm it or them. Popularity band-wagoning (yeah, I made that up) is so common because it is easier for people to accept something as fact, especially those closest to you… once others have.

Needing acceptance is not the same as having to earn someone's buy-in". Yes, you will have to earn a position by way of an interviewer's cosign. Yes, you will have to earn a role through an audition process. Yes, you will have to sell your concept to an investor. Yes, you will have to intrigue the masses if you have a product or goal that depends on public buy-in. However, this chapter is about personal acceptance in areas of worth, value, skillset, and talent. The key that unlocks other people's buy-in only works after you have truly become good with being your authentic self. Accept your "isms". Think about the traits of a person that society has told you is considered cocky or arrogant. Pause. I hate these labels because people usually use them when they feel threatened or can't handle a person's confidence. Ok I'm back. Think how that person always seems to win or get what they want. Most people trust, admire and accept confidence. I encourage all of my business development clientele to know their worth. I push them to find their own superpower and tell them to lead with it. Enter a business conversation knowing that your idea or product is good, and present it knowing that it will be liked, not hoping it will be accepted. If someone gives you something without accepting who you are with it, they can try to assume control in that area of your life. I remember getting jobs and eventually being given more leniency than my other colleagues. At the beginning, I would "start out how I knew I could hold out". A good friend told me years ago when she started working a job that she only started doing things a certain way based off her ability to sustain it. While I wanted the job, duh I applied, I didn't minimize myself. I went in knowing and being who I am, and what I would accept and deal with. This left me in power of the position and not a slave to it. I didn't need the job to validate my worth because I had determined that long before seeking employment. Learn to accept yourself! Know your strengths and weaknesses. Operate in your areas of greatness because those things are undeniable.

TRY THIS:

Consider the definition of you. How do you move, act, think, operate? Are you comfortable with those answers? If not, then those are the areas you should change. How would you want to change them? What would you change only because you feel inclined to? This is called self-work and is a must in the process of evolution. Don't allow the cop-out "this is just me" to prevent you from being honest with those less than stellar characteristics of yourself. Do the work to accept yourself, change those things that you have the ability to, and seek help in those areas that require assistance.

Don't, don't, don't change something about yourself that you love just because someone else doesn't but be sure that you actually love it...

Chapter 4

FALLBACK FROM PROCRASTINATION

There is no such thing as the perfect time…ever! The perfect time to move, the perfect time to try. Listen: it-doesn't-exist. Period. There is always some dynamic or detail that could be better. I consult with so many people that end up doing nothing because of self-delay. Many "thinkers" get stuck planning and never reach the action phase. The hardest thing to do is to get started and stay on task with your deadlines. In this day of everybody being "woke," could it be you haven't fulfilled your dreams because you are still asleep? Dreams stay in that form if you are resting. Get to work! Time is not on your side because it is consistent even when you are not. Set goals and make a to-do list. That list should change weekly because of the completion of items on it and the addition of new ones. If it is not, then you are procrastinating, or you've missed some necessary steps to add to your to-do list. Don't let your wait and preparation period morph into stagnation. Get it done!

TRY THIS

Consider, what is the true seed of your procrastination? I recognized in writing this book I was procrastinating completion because I didn't want to do the work I knew would be necessary to market it. Be honest with yourself and meet the delaying stronghold head-on. Once you have, you will see a return to progress and completion.

Chapter 5

FALLBACK FROM TRYING TO PROVE WHO YOU ARE

…to everyone.

Including your loved ones.

Everyone has a purpose unique to them which gives them a clarity nobody else can have for it and the path towards it. Trying to prove your purpose distracts you from simply living in it by wasting time and energy to convince people of something they shouldn't be able to weigh in on. Like Keke Palmer infamously said, "The gag is, you weren't there… so you don't know". Which means, you have no say so on that. People will develop their own idea of who you are based on little to nothing that you have actually done. Sometimes it's based on how they perceive you, life, their values and other times they've just chosen to believe rumors. Living in hiding or in defense of others perceptions doesn't do anyone any good. No matter what you say or do, people will believe what they want! I had an opportunity to work with Kanye West on a couple of live performances at the Hollywood Bowl during his 808 & Heartbreak album run. I remember going in with this idea about who he was and how he was going to act. Yes, I had my guard up! I must say that I left the experience with a completely different perspective of him. Even though he knew his reputation, he didn't come in the rehearsals trying to defend himself, his rumor or his character. Rather he operated in truth to his passions, and how he approached developing a vision.

Wasting time on anything else would've impacted the reason we were there. That vision-show was epic and so was the process. My experience of him was completely different from my expectations of him. I would have missed the blessing of that interaction had I not been open to receive him organically. Furthermore, when the opportunity to work with him again with the Sunday Service Collective presented itself, I eagerly said yes to one of the dopest experiences of my career at the time. While working with Sunday Service, the media had a field day spreading rumors. I learned how to truly ignore others' opinions especially when they are sourced from nothingness, steeped in opinions and fueled by agendas often misunderstood by the general public they are meant to affect. As experienced through people like Michael Jackson, Winona Ryder, Bill Cosby, Lindsey Lohan, Russell Simmons, Martin Luther King Jr., and a whole bunch of other public figures, despite all the great things they accomplished, their legacy stories are always accompanied by the inclusion of their less than great moments. Yet still they trod. In a lot of cases, society will redefine a person's entire being and life off one mishap. Truthfully, everyone has them, and no one wants to be judged or limited by them, but people still use them to define and minimize others. Sometimes it doesn't have to even be a mistake you made as we know ulterior motives don't need obvious or clear cause. Other times, people tend to criticize what they don't understand, are threatened by or triggered from. The need for others to agree helps validate their actions by overshadowing their motives. They want to sleep at night... Yes, misery still loves company. People choose to believe what they want to support their actions. Besides, drama and mess are always the juicer stories. Something about painting someone else in a bad light, especially when they are intimidated by them, helps the gap of where they are; not feel so big. Some would rather debate if NBA legend Lebron James is a better basketball player than NBA Legend Michael Jordan than to give him kudos for the school he opened for at-risk children and any of the other things he has accomplished. He doesn't succumb to the noise to prove or argue that he is a better player nor beg for acknowledgment for the other things. He has removed the need for public buy in to live in his true purpose and character?

Live in your truth and do epic shit! Your less-than-great moments make you human. Find inner peace, get up, and keep on living. Now I'm going to say this and I'm sure you are going to have some judgement, but roll with me, Donald Trump gets it. Love him or hate him most people can agree he is unapologetically him. He won the top position in America without trying to prove himself to be anything else other than who he is.

TRY OR THINK THIS

How many times have you changed someone's perception of you? You probably haven't by anything you've tried to explain. People's interaction and experience of you is valid. If you want to change how someone sees you, show up differently; consistently. At some point, accept when someone has reached their pinnacle idea of you. Even if they are completely wrong, there is nothing you can do to change that. You will encounter those that have developed a perception of you without interacting with you. Move around. If they decide to change their thoughts of you, they will do it on their own. It is at that time that you get to determine how your experience of them impacts your interaction too.

Chapter 6

FALLBACK FROM THE SHAME OF PRIDE

Let me start by saying the way we define words is the cause of a lot of misunderstandings and miscommunications. The English language has so many different meanings for the same word. Coupled with intent, tone, and delivery, it's a wonder anyone ever truly understands what the next person is trying to verbally convey. Many words have double meanings, and unfortunately the popular inclination is to assume the negative one first, especially via text. Don't assume, get clarity. Before you get into a conversational debate with someone, make sure you both agree on the definitions of the words or topics you're debating.

Moving on... Pride. First, redefine words like pride, humble, bold, confidence, high self-esteem, determination, swag, and relentlessness. Society, and the church, has added such negative connotations to these words that are some of the necessary traits of an innovator, leader, thought provoker and overall successful person. It is no wonder so many people aren't. The very traits they need to adapt and perfect are things they have been told to avoid.

Pride, by its true definition, is a good thing.

Pride:

1. (N) A feeling or deep pleasure or satisfaction derived from one's own achievements, the achievements of those with whom one is closely associated, or from qualities or possessions that are widely admired.

2. (V) Be especially proud of a particular quality or skill as in he prided himself on his accomplishments.

-Webster Dictionary

What is there to be ashamed of?

I hated being called "uppity" because of the nasty snarl and tone people had when they said it. I asked someone, "what does that mean really?" They replied, "you are picky and particular!" So! What's wrong with that? Everyone has preferences. It dawned on me that when someone's "picks" are different from another's', they can become intimidated and insecure if they perceive yours as better. To get rid of that feeling, they attack to turn pride in your choice into a character flaw in their trigger.

English and its double meanings for words leave room for various interpretations and understandings. For example, On one hand you hear people say, "have pride in your work" or "walk in with pride." On the other, you hear people say "don't act too proud". The latter is a method of control and minimization which confuses the definition of the word and causes some to never experience the reward of feeling the true sense of pride. Choose positive definitions of words versus accepting negative ones. Shed the social stigma that pride is a characteristic of an asshole. People that can't take your pride, may covet or hold insecurities in your areas of excellence. Don't get mad, they just can't help themselves. Since pride is defined as doing something with excellence or at your level best, and laced with confidence, there is nothing to be ashamed of. You should operate in such a manner and be proud of everything you do if you do it with pride. There is nothing wrong with knowing and walking in your worth. Minimizing yourself only stifles your purposed. Trying to get others to understand it and shrinking for their comfort, is a mishandling of self. Don't fumble your potential.

Be bold. Be confident. Be relentless. Be prideful.

TRY THIS

Make a list of things about yourself that make you happy or feel good; like a trait, experience, action, or feature. Recite this list to yourself once a day. Call it self-building manifestations. Love on yourself and the things that you are good at. This will also help you walk with authority into your field of excellence and purpose. These strengths need your pride to keep them strong. When something on that list begins to fall from reality, decide if you want to keep it or not. If you do, you know what to work on. As you grow, always add to this list. Don't stress trying to complete it as there are limitless things about yourself that you should be proud of. Stand in pride!

Chapter 7

FALLBACK FROM LIVING IN BOXES

Boxes are meant to control and confine. Well yeah that's not profound in this themed writing of achieving greatness. But, I'm not saying that boxes are bad. I am saying that staying or living in one theoretically is. Here's the thing, everything has a purpose, including a box. Great things come in boxes. In most cases, the box is a necessary container to get its contents delivered to the appropriate recipient. You may not be received until you have done your time in a box. Even a priceless piece of jewelry comes in a box. In most cases, a damaged box reduces the value of the entire package. A box is a place of protection. It is necessary for growth, privacy and transportation. The very boxes most parents place around children in the form of upbringing and home training stem from what their level of experiences and attempt to protect and teach you from them. They don't want you to experience damage. In that way, boxes can be comfortable because of their protective purpose of keeping things or people out. But be careful! After a while, that protection can evolve into a hideout reinforced by fear aka a stronghold. Don't let the distraction of comfort leave you vulnerable to suffocation. A box is still a box and you will shortly run out of air! You may find yourself in a box from your childhood, but like Jack, at some point you need to pop out of it. Boxes can be dark and prevent you from seeing that you have made it to your next destination. A savvy person knows how to allow a box to fulfill its delivery purpose without overextending their stay upon arrival. They even know when and how to get into a new box for delivery to a new destination. Once there, they quickly abandon the confines of it as well. We grow. Why would one box from a previous model of yourself be able to contain a newer version? It shouldn't. If you are ever evolving and emerging brand new, your value deserves journey protection. It deserves a new box.

Boxes in the form of stereotypes and social norms are meant to categorize people and control them. This isn't a box for delivery this is a cell for restriction. Though shaped the same, the purposes are completely different. The Bible itself speaks of the free-will of man, and quickly lays a roadmap of don'ts designed to control just how free that will should be.

HUH???

Man edited can be man confusing. Anyway, it then spotlights rebels that did not live in their boxes, from Moses to Jesus, only to be supported and celebrated by God. Where's the lie? Freedom is a gift from God. Why would you let man, and their adaptation of God's word, take it away?

A dive into the Box of the Black Man.

The socially restricting and stereotypical boxes for Black men during childhood and adolescence stifle many positive achievements outside of sports and entertainment. When was that seed planted? Some of the Black male boxes of defining masculinity prevents them from developing quality relationships, communicating, showing emotion, having compassion, being visibly happy, subscribing to sciences and education, having to walk or talk a certain way and more. As a child and adolescent, these boxes emasculate any Black male that operates in any of those manners. They are labeled, ridiculed, and encouraged to turn away from those behaviors. While those that chose to stay within the box are celebrated. What's sad is those behaviors are essential tools for someone to be a leader, entrepreneur, enter a healthy relationship, be creative, live an overall happy life and more. Many men don't develop these tools because of these boxes, and the fear of being labeled gay. What's worse is that the child once celebrated for not embracing those skills opting to wear a scowl, slack in scholastic achievement, adapt a "hard" mantel, objectify women, bully others, focus on sports alone, communicate disrespectfully and walk, talk, and dress "hard", later becomes labeled a thug or angry black male and then become targeted and killed by others like him or find police threatened by them. What's sad is acceptance of this image is so common and highly promoted that the Black men that don't subscribe to it still find themselves guilty of it. I found myself challenged with this because I too suffered from the charge of trying to fit in to avoid ridicule growing up. It became a harder revelation for me when I found myself doing this same thing to my own son. While being so quick to fuss and tell him what he shouldn't do, I was forgetting to check into what he naturally wanted to do. It's a person's natural ability that leads to their ultimate purpose. Killing the root of who a person is ends their ability to be unique and impactful. I was teaching my son how to hide the same way I was programmed to. My shame came when I remembered saying that I'd never do that to my children. He was 13 when I realized I had. Tear these walls down. This isn't a box that other groups have to live in. Even the playful demeanor and relationship that White men have with each other is accepted and often expected. Black men who display that demeanor with each other are usually scrutinized and chastised because of it being perceivably soft. Yeah there goes that gay thing again. In case you haven't figured it out, the word gay is used as a synonym of bad in the Black culture. Everything negative or perceivably weak is called gay. Those same actions are not considered as such in other cultures. When did a walk, talk, actions or showing of emotion determine sexual interest? I'd venture to say it stems from a mentality of masculinity beaten into the psyche of our enslaved ancestors or perhaps the reality that former slave owners would emasculate their male slaves by raping them anally. It makes sense in theory. Break the man's characteristics for compassion so they are nothing but pure raw work animal brutes; trained to "work and fuck." Anything that resembled weakness is beat out of them. This also led to a disassociation of marriage from sex as the house wives snuck to have sex with their servants before sending them back to their wives.

A theory; here we are years later still operating, as a community, in the programming that was set in place years ago to control us. Why does the Black culture continue to put their sons in that box and expect a different type of man to emerge from it? Name one current Black man who the Black community unanimously agrees is a great leader without pause or character damaging edits.

Now try to name one Black Woman that the community accepts as a leader and great example. Imbalanced? This is not by accident.

The walls of social boxes of any kind, for any group, are so layered that they are hard to break. It is left up to the individual to break them, which can prove to be challenging. First, they must recognize the presence of the box, and determine if they have outgrown it. Those who break the restrictions of them can experience the fullness of life, but should be careful not to repeat the cycle by putting their children or others into the very boxes they shed. While I certainly do believe that there is a time and place for everything, I believe even stronger that one should always be his/her/their authentic self. No one ever celebrated someone who was afraid to let their greatness shine. Besides, boxes are not a one-size-fit-all, so at some point of growth, you will have to break out of it. The people still living in a box you once shared and the ones that put you in it will not be immediately happy about your emergence. But this is about you, right?

Sledgehammer to the walls, break the box down.

TRY THIS

What unexplored dreams, goals and desires do you have? Why? If your answers is because you think it is taboo, was told not to, or feel ashamed to, then you are living in a box. It is time to return yourself to the liberated imagination of your dreams. Make a plan and live free! A caged life ain't ever been a happy life. It damn sure doesn't get you to the platform of purpose the inner real you so desperately desires. You owe it to yourself. Get the sledgehammer. Break the box!

Chapter 8

FALLBACK FROM FEARING THE UNKNOWN

What do you fear? Many of us won't answer that question. Some of us can't for a lack of self-evaluation. Others won't because they've been programmed to believe fear makes them weak. You don't realize just how weak you are until fear busts you upside your head unexpectedly. Some experience as a panic or anxiety attack. I experienced it while in Mexico working on a project. Out of nowhere, the crippling thought of being alone and not fulfilling my purpose laid me out! We all fear something, and not knowing what that is leaves us vulnerable to being consumed by it. If you know your fears, you can work on not letting them control or surprise you. Not knowing them can stop you in your tracks when inevitably revealed. After calling a close friend, Nusie, who helped me breathe, calm down, process and get up again, I began to implement action and changes that would thwart the reality of those fears to manifest.

Many people fear the unknown. History has shown us the horrible way humans deal with the unknown or misunderstood; we kill. Be it a dream, a goal, a reputation, home or even a life; the need to eradicate it almost always reveals itself. Imagine the many possibilities that have been terminated because of their uncommonness. Don't be the person that kills someone's potential because you don't know or understand something. I meet so many people who have never tried a new place. traveled, explored something, or met someone new because they didn't "know" it. You enter this world knowing nothing, yet as a child you instinctively desired to explore things; even when your parents told you no. Why as an adult would you limit your crusade for explorative experiences to those you embarked upon as a child? Return to your natural desire to explore. Many people miss out on some of the greatest places, experiences and moments life has to offer all because they cannot get out of their comfort zone. Ironically, they aren't even that comfortable because it is a zone someone else put them in (See Chapter 7, it just might be a box). Their fear of planes or boats, because they don't know what could happen, cancels out travel abroad. Their decision to only eat what they ate growing up causes them to miss out of some of the most amazing culinary delights the world has to offer. Their inability to meet and mingle with other races and cultures leaves them stuck with small life perspectives. They miss out on the true joy of living because they're stuck in an inherited comfort zone. Most comfort zones are constructed from the boxes that were made for us by our parents, government, religions and other outside influences. Advancements in every field of human endeavor have been made since forever because someone dared to try something different. Fear of the unknown shouldn't have the power to stifle your life. Don't leave the questions you have unchallenged. If you question it, so do others. Why shouldn't you be the one to provide the answer to it? Get out there, explore, and experience. Your exploration may lead you to a discovery that could change the world and life as we know it; in the best of ways. Life is all about experiences. Ready to live?

TRY THIS

==

What were the last 5 new things you have tried? Make a list of the 5 new things. Write down why you haven't tried them. What is a reoccurring block that stifles your ability to explore? Daily manifest that you are the opposite of that. Return to your list and set some timeline goals to try them.

Chapter 9

FALLBACK FROM DOUBT

A t first read of this chapter's title, you probably assumed that I am referring to self-doubt and yes, you should fallback from that too. Believe in yourself... yada yada, all of that is good. However, in this case I am referring to the doubt of not trusting others. What relationship and benefit from it are you missing because of your trust issues? How are you living? Are you trustworthy? Sometimes we don't trust because we know that we shouldn't be trusted. Trauma.

While we must try our best to protect ourselves from ill intentions that other people can sometimes have, no man is an island. Everyone isn't: guilty, trying to take advantage, run game on you, or your hater. This is the truth, regardless of any previous let-downs or burns you have experienced. There are many people in the world with pure intentions. We would readily know what the intentions were if we were honest about them out the gate. I understand this is not common, but the assumption of the alternate can prevent a partnership that could change your life. Success and enjoyment often come from effectively partnering with other people. In many cases, this isn't with people you've already known. It's common to hear someone say they are closer to their chosen family than their biological ones, and they work better with non-family members. However, history reveals the opposite. Family dynasties have yielded some of the most successful collaborations. It's interesting to me how we hold people we are in proximity with, who have never harmed, and we enjoy being around to a higher standard of judgment, guard and suspicion than we do those that have consistently done us wrong, or we don't know at all. Yes, do your filtering and pay attention to the signs that reveal who people are, but know a crippling doubt of others will prevent you from working that one investor, partner, or connect, aka the plug, that will get you to the next level. Figure a balance between trust and test by doing your due diligence with all parties! Before you start partnering or meeting people, protect yourself. Make great passwords, copyright and or patent your ideas; make your personal belongings secure and safeguard your possessions. Do this for both business and personal interactions. People can only access what you allow. Give access in due time as opposed to not at all. There's a song that says, "No New Friends" that is catchy, but quite stifling to a person's growth. New friends yield new experiences, opportunities, and self-awareness. If old friends were the key, you'd already be where you want to be. Unless you have influential friends that for whatever reason deny collaborations. In that case, are y'all truly friend? *Shrug*, sorry Drake. Catchy songs versus how an artist really thinks and lives are two different things. I'm sure Drake has mastered the art of new ventures and partnerships that have yielded new friends; it's evident in his success and continued growth. He also has some longtime friends that serve their purposes as well which means, it's not an all one way or nothing at all concept. I wish the masses, especially Black people, really understood that. Some of our old friends tend to have the hardest time accepting our new greatness and allowing us to grow and change, even though we want them to be the first and biggest source of support. I must say that we own some responsibility for that because often we shrink when we are around them. We don't want them to know that we have changed. The fear of losing a lifelong friend makes us subconsciously desire to be perceived and subsequently received the same way. Doubt can't exist amongst facts there must be shades of grey. Take inventory in the facts of what someone says and how they interact with you, not someone else's experience of them. Anyone who doesn't truly support growth or change will display it. So don't miss out on necessary connectivity. Biblically speaking, it was the first request of Man; companionship. Without trying, you will never know. Give people a controlled chance aka benefit of the doubt.

TRY THIS

Write out your goals. Write out who in your network/you know could help you achieve them. Any open slots or slots filled with people you haven't spent any time connecting or conversing with is where you need to begin. Trust safely. Put so much focus and strength in the positive and the goal that it becomes necessary to achieve. Allow the fear of not achieving that goal to eclipse the fear of doubting it.

Chapter 10

FALLBACK FROM PERPETUATING YOUR STEREOTYPE

J ust because someone says it, doesn't mean you have to manifest it.

All Black people aren't lazy, mad and late. All White people aren't conniving, manipulative and elitist. All Asian people aren't misogynistic, opportunist, and submissive; and all Hispanic people aren't bad drivers, ill-tempered, and cheap manual laborers. You do not have to walk in a lane someone paved for you. Eliminate the "They-Sayers" along with the nay-sayers. They-Sayers are such a powerful group of people in the sense that nobody can tell you who the hell "they" are, but everybody is living up to the standards in which "they" set. So, why live under the guidelines of the "they" that you never have and never will meet? I go into more detail about this in Chapter 24. Go be uniquely you, uninhibited by stereotypes. Stereotypes can be negative or positive, but either way they don't automatically apply to everybody and everything. Be it perceivably good or bad, do you, no matter what your ethnic stereotype is. All Black people aren't entertainers, athletic, or able to cook. All White people aren't executives, leaders, or wealthy (nor do they automatically tip well). All Asians aren't smart, business-minded, or model minorities. All Hispanics aren't good with their hands, curvaceously sexy, or Spanish speakers. Not only are the stereotypes simply untrue, they limit your potential. If you only subscribe to the things you are "supposed" to be good at based off your culture, what talents are you not exploring? When I first started singing R&B music, I was told that I wasn't urban enough in the way that I pronounced my words, sung certain lines, or penned song topics. I allowed people to tell me what the genre of music was supposed to discuss when genres simply define how a song sounds based off chord structure, musicality and vocal approach. To be honest, I only chose R&B as a genre because at that age, if you didn't sing gospel and you were Black you automatically placed in that category. I had a son at 21, I pledged Kappa Alpha Psi, I was living and wanted to sing things other than Jesus died. So R&B it was… I begin to conform, or at least tried to and failed miserably, to fit in a commercial box of what an R&B artist was supposed to be. This never worked for me. Once I abandoned the stereotypes and got back to creating the music I felt, how I felt it and stayed true to it, I became impactful as an artist. It took me years because I wanted to work the formula towards success that I had been taught. You can see the growth and feel the authenticity between my "Think DeP Reloaded" LP," Red Light Pt. II", "Fallback" and my most recent projects, "This Shit Can't Wait" & "Edibles & Elevation." It's sad to see so many people accepting and living under the definitions of these stereotypes, especially minorities as we have some of the most crippling negative stereotypes. Interestingly, many White people will deny their negative stereotypes publically and not showcase those behaviors and often deny them. Although in recent times, that is changing some as we are starting to see a lot of them BOLDLY walking around with their "Hoods Off" lately. BUT, that group still denies their actions and hide it under confusion, false tears and gaslighting via hero complexes when questioned so the next thought still applies. How often do you hear them talking about their less-then superior stereotypes? They rarely showcase themselves like that in conversation, jokes, film, and to the public in general. When there is an act of terror executed by a White person, they are presented to the public differently, including the picture used on media outlets. When hanging with my Caucasian friends, they privately disclose their believed insecurities or negative stereotypes. I can respect that because I don't think there is a need to elevate negativity. They have done an excellent job with keeping their less-than stellar members and short-comings from being the automatic perception and representation of them as a group. Minorities, however, have seemingly adapted the negative cultural stereotypes given to them, and use them as a framework for expected and appropriate behavior within their own cultures. As of late, I recognize more and more how quick certain groups create content that popularizes stereotypes for likes and monetization. At the cost of the culture, they opt to make a spectacle and seemingly authenticate false behaviors and traits that teach others what to expect of them, which doesn't accurately depict the majority. Because of the visibility of that stereotype and financial award perceivably obtained by personifying it, the next generation desires it and so they adapt it as a new cultural norm reversing the progress their ancestors worked so hard to achieve. Growing up, I remember being told to keep the family business in the family. It isn't being ashamed or denial of possible hints of truth, but it is controlling how people perceive, respect and what they expect of you. Why feed the very stereotypes that people use to think less of you?

TRY THIS

What stereotypes of yourself do you find yourself personifying? Are they really you? If not, STOP IT. You can help change the narrative and expectation of your people.

Chapter 11

FALLBACK FROM MAKING PLANS CONTINGENT ON THE BUY-IN OF OTHERS

How many times have your plans changed because you were waiting on someone? From the small to the big, productivity can always be stifled by waiting on someone else. Many people have a hard time completing things for themselves let alone anyone else. Why would they have a stronger conviction towards completion for you? Ask yourself, what can you do alone to get closer to accomplishing your goal? You dreamed your dream, so it's not necessary to share it with others before beginning to work on it. Everyone can see the potential in a good idea, but that doesn't mean they can or will help you execute it. Guess what? While you were dreaming, so was everyone else...about something completely different. A few people have had the same dream or similar idea, forcing the matter of who is going to do it first. Remember the old saying, "there's nothing new under the sun" – unknown. Things that are destined to happen, will happen.

A small-scale example, making travel plans with a group is always harder than booking a solo trip. Why? Financial restrictions, timing, different interests, purpose, preferences, and various definitions of fun are just a few reasons. People move, feel and think differently, and that doesn't make anyone wrong. The revelation of those differences can question the inclusion. Since everyone is entitled to their opinion, who's preferences should yield?

On a much larger scale, building a business team is extremely difficult. Though teamwork really does make the dream work, building one is a tedious and delicate process. Finding team members who identify a common goal, mutual interest in the business success but not wanting to have the exact same position is key. Consider a great team can be comprised of people you haven't even met yet. You can have numerous people around and not have anyone that has the capacity to fill the missing gap. Some that have the capacity to, may not believe in you or want to partner in that way. Don't force business buy-ins from personal ties! So, you need some initial help and only have your known connections? If you must, start with your circle but keep it in perspective. Here's how: Do not approach your close network for long-term or permanent positions within your business structure unless you imagined the idea together. Relationships will encourage people to help you for a short time. After a while, especially if success isn't immediate, their initial excitement and support will fade. Do not let this impact your personal relationship, in other words, "don't forget to come and pick up your feelings"- J. Sullivan.

Once you identify the needs, begin to save and build your staffing budget. Pay people to do what you can't. Hiring people is a great way to have them commit to completion as opposed to relying on your relationship. You control the narrative on deadline, details, process and quality. Hiring draws a clear line between relationship and responsibility. Once completed, you also maintain ownership of the concept and idea. Ownership is the key to wealth, future savvy business options and ultimate control over your idea and intellectual property! Be the principal player in your plans. Making plans that will break down if someone doesn't do their part is the best way to ALMOST do a whole lot.

TRY THIS

Look at your goals and To-Do List. Break down the list into specific things that need to happen in chronological order. Determine which things you can do on your own and do them. List the remaining things, find out the market value for them and create a budget for them. HIRE OUT! When hiring make sure you consider quality, experience, and execution over quick access and relationship. There are several apps and programs that have budget-friendly contractors for work such as graphic design, reports, financial analyst, social media content creation and more.

Chapter 12

FALLBACK FROM TRYING TO PROVE YOUR POINT AND LISTENING JUST TO RESPOND

DON'T...

Nobody cares! Everyone has an opinion, and thinks theirs is right, look at social media... People present themselves as experts after building their opinions and conclusions from content they have found on other people's social media' pages. This has happened with elections, Covid19 vaccinations, investments, other people's business, and so on. Then enter the comments, which many of us are there for, and you can see a whole lot of people just want to argue and are anti. In this scenario, it's because most people are arguing opinions as opposed to facts. In the few cases where factual data is shared, current trends of trolling and being anti have given users the false idea that they are right no matter what. So, they boldly enter the fray, supported by the inevitable few that agree with them or have other motives, just to spew their opinion. Often, they begin to look foolish and compromise their credibility on anything. Don't become categorized as one of those. Your goals, jobs, and even purpose can be put in jeopardy. It just isn't worth it. Some people create posts just to start online debates. Learn from this. A person's post on social media is their opinion, and they are entitled to it. Unless they asked you a question, it is simple to just read it and slide on by. You can waste a whole lot of time and energy trying to get people to see your point. The thing is, they don't have to. If you're confident in your convictions, live in them. It's popular, but you don't always have to clap back, nor do you have to respond. Your clap back reveals your loss of control, which is what a lot of people want you to do. You lose focus on the point and so does the observer as they get distracted by the arguing of semantics. My fellow Spet 4 Virgo and previous boss, Beyoncé said it well, "best revenge is your paper." Make money, not noise.

The power of TRUE conceding is enormous! One person said, "Silence is a powerful response in many cases." In business, let the customer be right. You may earn their loyalty because of how you handled the situation and them. Taking the loss (the L), shouldn't be considered a bad things as ultimately, you need the customer for a successful business. There's always a lesson in interaction with customers of all types, mastering a handing of each of them will have a much bigger reward than some temporary showcase of power. We live in a society where being right seems to carry more weight than treating people right; until it backfires. Is your business worth the gamble?

If you stay open, your convictions and points will either be confirmed or transformed as you live. They are for you. They should be the framework of how you choose to live. Trying to prove your point to others typically leads to an argument and even if you are right, most people won't confess that to you. They'll just lure you in, change the main topic, and you'll find yourself arguing about something completely irrelevant; leaving you tired from the energy exerted which could've been used to simply live. Many people listen just to respond because they have a need to be right or they may be driven by the desire to prove you wrong. They use supporting arguments and examples that ultimately divert the topic, and boom, you've lost your point anyway. I've had several people tell me that I think I'm always right and that others believe I am too. I corrected them. I feel secure in my convictions and beliefs, I seek to support them with fact and am readily willing to change my perspective if proven incorrect. I always speak from that mindset. The truth is, I am not always right, nor do I aim to be. I am always confident that I have done the due diligence in supporting my thoughts while accepting that I could be wrong. I speak definitively about things I am 95% sure about. I also ask for clarity on things that I do not know or am unsure about, intentionally putting myself in a position of forever learning. Not speaking on those things keep me from speaking from the wrong side of a topic. Though bigger than being right or wrong, I understand the concept of learning, listening, and adapting my stance on anything I dare to converse about. I avoid arguing for that reason. My approach to conversational debate is to express my stance and support it by all I know and believe, while listening to an opposing one and being fully prepared to embrace that logic to change mine when appropriate. It's not about winning! It's about mutual growth opportunity and understanding the role of "The Giver" and "The Receiver" of knowledge always rotates. I have a friend who does not express herself well when trying to convey her feelings. When she tries to make a point, she can never support it. She ultimately gets frustrated which results in her yelling and cursing simply because she recognizes that she's not supporting her thoughts the way she wants to. She also hates for people to confuse her intentions because of her struggles with effective communication. While we all can become emotionally tied to a topic, it is our job to keep our emotions intact and accept that though deeply felt, they may not be factual. There's a defense statement used as a mechanism I describe as a "fake yield" ... "Let's just agree to disagree." That statement is mostly used as a cop-out. It stops conversation and is usually presented by someone who has hit a wall in trying to express himself or support her point, but unwilling to believe they may need to change their outlook. It is especially obvious when that statement is used before the other party has even had a chance to state and support their stance. That person is simply saying, "I don't care what you will say, I want to believe it this way and will do so no matter what." End this conversation! In a past relationship, I dated someone who was unable to "use the right words" and so they would internalize their own conclusions and take them as fact. There was no way to resolve things because I found myself always checking, pulling for them to communicate, guessing what they meant and dealing with the fact that they felt spoken down to because I didn't face the same communication challenges they did. It ended. If people can't accept or they can't "take you", they can't truly receive anything from you. It doesn't matter how you shape or support your thought. In that relationship, they needed me to be the villain because if it wasn't me it would have to be them.

Many of the social and economic discussions on race, wealth, laws and more are not about being right but about how the outcome effects the individual. You then have someone arguing a moral stance while another is defending a system that benefits them. Right doesn't win cases or arguments. Determining right from wrong isn't hard. Most people know when they are technically wrong, and often argue the obvious to justify their actions to support their beneficially right. This is what makes right and wrong subjective and an easy catalyst to argue. If someone believes they are right and are unwilling to change that, there is nothing you can say or do that will convince them they aren't. Utilize your convictions to motivate you to live your best life, and operate to the best extent of your ability, morals and beliefs. If your passion is to impact change in policy or societal thought, gear up strategically, test your hypothesis, study it's history, find your audience, build a platform and get active spreading your message. You will then have the power to convince others to share your viewpoint. The question then becomes, how do you get your influence and credibility up? The answer is by operating and doing work that becomes your proof of thought and its impact all while avoiding the need to argue or prove why.

Supporting your point vs. listening to someone just to respond.

- Explaining yourself and your views can be done so without arguing their value as more or less than another's.

- Listening just to respond can happen in verbal, written and online communication.

The energies and intent are different. In some cases, when people are trying to support their point, they are passionate about their stance, excited to share their findings, believe they are right and want to hold strong to their deep personal conviction because they have done what they consider the work to support it requires. When listening to respond, a person is often trying to win an argument, doesn't care if they are being rational or logical, and disregard the other person's input. Disagreements don't have to evolve into arguments, but often do when the parties involved seek to solely justify their stance. Don't approach conversation as an opportunity to win. Thinking along those terms indicates that someone must be a loser, and so the race is on! The desire to be right can be so strong you can miss out on what the other person is saying. The other person, who justifiably has a difference of opinion, can say something that benefits you and your perspective. The person that is unwilling to expand his perception is limited yet comfortable in the blissful existence that ignorance creates. Successful people seek opportunities to grow and surround themselves with others who are equally or more successful and knowledgeable than they are! I personally love to debate as an exchange of ideas and opportunity to grow. I only debate peers of the understanding of debate. You cannot grow if you cannot hear and accept that your opinion can be wrong. If you are unwilling to hear, don't engage in conversation with others. A conversation is a verbal exchange between two or more people. If ideas and thoughts are not mutually exchanged, it isn't a conversation it is a lecture.

Dear friend, you don't have to respond to everything, but you should be able to accept hearing and reading anything. Take what you want from what you hear or read and leave the rest behind. Arguing about it has no reward and is an exhaustion of effort and energy.

TRY THIS

Accept your points as your truth. Avoid explaining and move in silence. Moving in silence helps alleviate the need to explain your actions. Ask yourself, what aren't you doing because someone else thinks you shouldn't? Practice effective communication skills. Gage how many times you've ever changed your stance? How many times do you ask for information or an opinion without the need to counter respond? If you find yourself constantly defending yourself, could you be keeping the wrong company or could your actions and thoughts use some reevaluating?

Chapter 13

FALLBACK FROM TAKING ON OTHER PEOPLE'S SHIT

Don't be the person that doesn't like someone or something just because someone else doesn't. You could miss out on the one thing that'll be life transformative in the best of ways all because you heard it wasn't good. "No love, that ain't good." Groupthink has always been a thing, but with today's society of acceptance, social media, and the thirst for likes, it has become a contagious epidemic. If "they" like it, you're supposed to. If "they" don't like it, then you shouldn't either. HUH? They call it cancel culture now and frankly, some of the wrong things and people have been cancelled. It's interesting which things have not been... Some argue that Republican Liz Cheney's removal from the GOP because of her stance on what she considered lies; was wrong. Agreeing with her or not, a group of people chose to remove her because of her opinion. Some did so because the majority did even after applauding her stated opinion. The ability to vote anonymously allowed them to unite the group mission without having to accept the public scrutiny and responsibility of their thoughts, alignment and action. If individually charged, uncoached and their stance publicly revealed, I wonder to what degree they would've aligned. A trending thought doesn't always mean it's good. We see this in the entrepreneurial world too. Many of us choose to publically share, comment, and like on social media based off of a number of variables well outside of the fact that the content actually resonates with us. Even down to who we follow and visibly interact with, some don't want to appear aligned with certain people for perception purposes because they don't want to compromise the brand they are building. Others may not want to shoulder any backlash for connectivity to a person or idea that may conflict the buy in of a certain audience. A few communicate with "controversial friends" via DM because they don't want others to know they are affiliated. The list goes on… Ultimately, they are making association decisions based on how other people perceive that individual or concept. They have bought into other people's shit and given it hierarchy in interaction.

But everybody is "woke" while making groupthink and sleepwalker decisions of association. Taking on other people's shit is concluding or deciding a stance about someone or something based on someone else's.

You don't have to like or dislike anyone or anything just because someone close to you or the masses do. In addition to fake-liking stuff, some people take on other people's mess, drama and issues. I've met people that take a vegan lifestyle because it's a trend, only to learn their body was not only allergic to the new diet they forced themselves to consume, but medically, they needed meat protein. For the vegan that needs, or simply wants to live that lifestyle for his or her own reasons, kudos. As for me, I like my chicken, pork, beef, broccoli, green beans, eggs, milk, cheese and everything else in between that Pastor Shirley Ceaser listed a few years ago; minus the Ram. However, you can miss me with mayo, onions, organ meats, and a whole list of other stuff. You get the point lol. To each their own. After all, it's their choice and not yours. Just make sure to make decisions based on how you feel versus how someone else does. Your lifestyle doesn't need a popular title for it to be the right one for you.

Now why did I use the word "shit"? Shit, in this context, is equivalent to waste. Waste is something the body disposes of because it doesn't need it and would do it harm if it couldn't get rid of it. Why would you pick that up and consume it? There are a lot of shitty behaviors that people pick up; being messy, having a bad attitude, uncontrollable and detrimental drug use, abusive actions, being inconsiderate, habitual lying, self-victimizing and more. Humans naturally adapt and learn through experiences. Basically, we pick up things that we encounter. Most times it's unconscious. The problem is that we pick up the bad just as easily as the good. Be sure you aren't picking up people's shit. It's hard enough to carry your own let alone someone else's. Stay in tune with who you are so you can recognize new behaviors and thought processes. Check them early! If you notice that you are beginning to take on someone else's behavior or mindset, determine if is truly a gem, or just another piece of…SHIT.

TRY THIS

Check into and worry about yourself. What are some of your hard stances in life? Why are they? Did someone tell you to take that stance? Do you get that gut feeling after saying or doing something that "wasn't really cool?" Is that stance something resonating within? Is society or a big group of people encouraging you to feel that way? Has media planted ideas and thoughts that you haven't researched for yourself? Did your parents instill their ideals so deep that you have adapted them as yours, unmodified? Think about that person or group of people you don't like. Why don't you? You will truly begin to live once you let go of the load you have been influenced to carry. Your path and YOUR story will not look like anyone else's.

Chapter 14

FALLBACK FROM GET-RICH-QUICK SCHEMES

D^{on't.}

OK really. IF YOU MUST, get in early, focus on the short game and get out. By the time the idea is trending, you are too late. Avoid including loved ones in the venture, a moral issue accompanies that as there is no guaranteed win in these scenarios. A win via this method requires several to lose; it's a numbers game so avoid involving including those you are close to. Here's a few reasons why: If they are in your circle, you all probably know the same people and so recruiting will stall. Second, you will feel responsible, or at least should, for helping them get their financial promise. Ask yourself, how long has this opportunity been out? Many get-rich-quick opportunities are labeled pyramid schemes. I don't believe the word scheme is the best to use because it hints at a negative intent of those who are participating. For most, they aren't intentionally trying to take advantage of you. . To a degree, they don't fully comprehend what it takes to keep the opportunity going. The word "scheme" is appropriate for those who knowingly recruit others under guise of it being guaranteed or that their earning potential is equal to theirs. Truth is, there are people that make a lot of money from these businesses. These are the people who start early and recognize when to move on to the next venture before complete saturation or don't internalize the potential loss of their downward line. This is why when you look at the earning-level graphics, it is shaped like a pyramid or smaller to bigger circles. Structurally, all businesses are technically set up this way. The CEO of a "legitimate" business plan always earns more than the hired workers at the bottom or outer rings. Recall the phrase, "last hired; first fired." The longer it takes for you to get in, the further away you are to actualizing the promise. There is no real winning when you arrive late to a played-out idea. Keep in mind; if you can get something quickly, you can lose it quickly. Make a plan for quick money.

Crowd Funding Tips:

- **Many people have experienced success with crowd funding options such as Go Fund Me campaigns. Before starting one there are a few things to consider. Have you invested in yourself? Why should anyone donate to your goal when you haven't donated to it** yourself? My mom always told me that if you ask someone for help, especially in the form of money, you are also granting them permission to give their opinion or judgment...whether you asked for it or not. We all have experienced a person borrowing $20 from us only to find out later that they are partying or doing something extra-curricular with it. No matter what the details, we can't help but think, "They're out partying on my $20", thus the slippery slope of crowd fund-think begins: "What are you doing with the money we gave you?" is in the back of the mind of everyone who donated.

- Crowd funding is a great tool and method, but if you are going to go the public crowd-funding route, make sure that you are posting yourself in a positive light that shows your need, allocation of your own and the donators' funds, grind, appreciation and eventually the results of the funding. Don't forget to give updates and deliver on what you have promised. Remain humble when needing help while making sure you are a valuable investment. If you chose to crowd fun, make sure you have very visible explanations of progress and plans/execution of the goal. If you are self or privately funded, you don't have to worry about this dynamic.

TRY THIS

Find your passion and work in it. Working in your passion keeps you happy which has a much bigger payback than any dollar could. Get involved with opportunities that align with things you are interested in and have realistic returns. If you want to build a group that everyone puts money in, create an exit plan for the "pot money" that doesn't involve further recruitment, like a business idea, plan or investment. This is how you leverage your circle and the accessible income to provide an additional one to the group.

Chapter 15

FALLBACK FROM BEING PETTY

What is being petty? Intentionally saying or doing something that makes fun, insults, judges or puts someone on blast; causing them to feel shame or discomfort. The key word is intentional because it has become a trend for people to categorize everything as being petty or another similar term, shady. Being blunt, truthful, direct, disliking or disagreeing with someone is not being petty or shady. Some use that term as a deflection. Instead of dealing with their truth, they'd rather attack your integrity to minimize the impact of what you have said. Pettiness lies within a person's intention, not someone else's interpretation. Pettiness is a personal acceptance of fact. You can't control how people will interpret your facial expressions, text tones, delivery, timing or the things you say in general, but you can control the reason or intentions from which they derive. For example, calling someone out about their breath, where other people can hear you and attempting to shame them for a laugh, is petty. Being taken by surprise by someone's breath, resulting in an involuntary facial expression where someone else happens to see it, isn't. Even if that person begins to laugh, that's not a moment you have to own as an act of being petty. Those who are intentionally petty do so trying to get a laugh, feel better about themselves, deflect from their weakness or believe it will get them accepted in a certain crowd. That is a form of bullying. There is a difference between agendas, playful rapport and situational reactions. If you can accept your intentions you can rest in your truth.

A dangerous example of being petty is doing something just because you can get away with it or to prove an unjustified point. One example is when people decide to call the police on minorities for anything just as a threat. Those who are petty have summoned the police for seeing them walking, barbequing, babysitting, sleeping, swimming, and even entering their own residence. Why subject someone to discomfort, harassment and possible escalation of harm or death because of your own insecurities, stereotypes, or fears when the outcome changes nothing? That type of pettiness is an outward expression of another deeper-rooted issue. Another example can be a judge's exaggerated or maximum sentencing for a verdict when dealing with one guilty party as opposed to another for the same infraction. This doesn't help society in any way but does perpetuate the idea of one group having more value and consideration than another. The chain reaction to that societal norm negatively impacts communities and their interactions with each other across the world. Thus, abused power = Petty.

Pettiness has selfish intent. Being petty distracts you from who you should be worried about…yourself. Be careful not to become so busy looking for someone else's shortcoming or mishaps to hide your own. If you cannot operate outside of pettiness, you should have your power restricted. Being petty is an insecure characteristic of the small. Is that you? If so, "why are you down there?" Thanks Whitney, RIP.

TRY THIS

Consider the point when you are about to do or say something that could impact someone else. If it is to benefit them, pull them to the side and tell them. If there is no point, it probably could go without being said or done. If the point is to check, shock, embarrass or "Boom", then expect Karma to be waiting outside for that ass. FOR. IT. COMETH!

Daily Affirmations

I am royalty.

I move with intention and integrity.

I am rewarded financially.

I will always have more money than I need.

I cannot help but to constantly attract money into my life.

I am equipped physically, emotionally, mentally and spiritually to achieve my
purposed call and handle the responsibility of that money.

I am healthy and whole.

I am in alignment with my higher self.

I am at peace.

Àse.

Photography by: Shon Fuller

Photography by: Wardell Malloy

Photography by: Wardell Malloy

Photography by: Jordyn Castillo

Chapter 16

Fallback from Pursuing the Wrong Target Audience

Let's talk business. There is a personal audience and a business one aka target audience. Thousands of entrepreneurs and brands make the common mistake of thinking people they are personally connected to is their target audience. They begin to promote a product, idea or concept that doesn't align with them and they don't value because they are not the targeted audience. If you've experienced this, frustration can quickly ensue as you feel your energy and resources depleting without any major yield, response, or acts of support from your circle. Just because someone is in your personal audience does not mean they will be part of your target audience.

A great product answers a need or desire. Determine what you have to offer, and who needs or wants it. That is how you determine and begin to build your target audience. This applies to everything from music to a sustainable backup battery. When you first began to build your business plan, you should identify your target population.

RE: Social Media Followers

> IF YOUR AUDIENCE IS MADE UP OF PEOPLE THAT FOLLOW YOU FOR ANY OTHER REASON THAN AN INTEREST IN YOUR BUSINESS OR PRODUCT, THEY ARE NOT YOUR TARGET AUDIENCE, NOR DO THEY OWE YOU INTEREST OR SUPPORT FOR IT.

This is a mistake we all can make initially because of the excitement of moving a dream into a reality. I did the same thing for years when it came to my music. I expected my friends, church circle, school colleagues and others I knew from my many walks of life to like, want, buy, and share my music. I should have been making music that was true to my heart, and finding the audience that had a desire to hear it. It wasn't until I did that that I finally started being successful in the music industry. I went from begging for support to needing help managing the demand for it. For years I was offended at people I knew not liking what I offered musically enough to support me the way I thought they should when the truth was, they didn't have to. Naturally, when people really like something, no matter who they are, they tell people about it and support it. If you find yourself putting too much energy into trying to convince people to support you, your focus may need to shift to what you are offering. This is not a minimization of what you have, but just an oversight of who you are offering it to, and how visible it is to those who may be interested. My personal social media accounts were initially made up of friends, family and many people that subscribed to me for my look, wit and career associations, not necessarily fans of my music. That reflected in the engagements for post about my music in comparison to other post. Add in social media's algorithms that control who sees what you share, even though they opted in to see it by befriending or following you, and you have major blocks affecting your reach to your targeted audience. When you decide to start a new business or promote a product, consider a new social media profile so you can develop a true target audience for that new offering.

Test your product and market. Poll your target audience to get feedback on your product. Is it complete? Does it meet the need? Is it too much? Does the cost appeal to your target audience? Does your product cause people to want to return? All of these questions are necessary to have a successful product. Be flexible. As time goes by, your audience and/or your product may have to evolve.

Now let's get personal. At the age of 35 I tried to date what the 25 year-old version of me said I wanted. I got exactly that. The problem was that the 35 year-old me was extremely different in the values, expectations, and experience department than my younger version. I hadn't upgraded my expectations to match my elevation. We were doomed to fail because I didn't target the right partnership for where I currently was mentally, financially, or emotionally. At the end of that, consideration and a secure attachment style entered the top of my list but wasn't something I ever thought necessary to include because the 25 version of me thought that was understood. Nothing is. Many people have an outdated laundry list of what their ideal mates and friends should look like, have and be, but never develop one of what they themselves should bring to the table. Doing so will automatically update your list. The more you bring, what you expect evolves. Is your offering in alignment with your expectation? Who is in your personal target audience, and can they trust you to be a supplier? If it is friendship or companionship, the supply must match the offering and mutually appeal. In other words, bring something to the table and make sure whatever you bring is appropriate to the type of table you demand and it's company.

In business or personal, your audience can change and consequently so must your targeting tactics. When Coca Cola decided to become a beverage brand, offering more than just cola, they expanded their target audience and developed tactics to reach them. As you grow, so will the size and diversity of your audience. Learn how to serve your audience by first mastering the ability to recognize it.

TRY THIS

Who needs what you have to offer? Identify and figure out how to reach them. Where are they? What else do they like? Why do they need it? Is anybody else offering a solution to this want/need? If so, what works and doesn't work for them? This is the way to build your unique buying and supporting audience. The response and buy-in will reveal if you have found your audience.

Spend less time trying to convince those in proximity and go find those in alignment. Ok bye.

Chapter 17

FALLBACK ON ALWAYS FINDING THE NEGATIVE

There are some people that focus on the negative aspects about everything. Those same people struggle to find the positive elements about anything! Some even take it on as their self-appointed duty to find the downside to "keep someone humble" or "keep them living in reality". What a sad sense of purpose to walk this life with. It isn't your job to locate or create negativity. In worse scenarios, they tend to make up negative things when there is nothing to be found. During one of my favorite performance experiences with Beyoncé at a Grammy Awards Ceremony, we sung "Precious Lord" for a few positive reasons. Her mother used to sing it to her as a child; she wanted to make a statement for the *Hands Up Don't Shoot* movement that was happening, hence the reason for having all male singers and hands up choreography added, and her own spiritual background. Having had the opportunity to work with her several times since' then It blew my mind to see how a certain group of people loudly begin to cloud the positive reasons for her choosing this song, electing to make up drama and lies that she was spiting another artist. I was so proud to be a part of this moment yet at the same time a high feeling of sadness and shame that this group would choose to block out a positive movement to find something negative to add to it. The sadness arrived because I understood that they had been programmed to think this way and I recognized just how much work, internal work, needed to be done. Though the performance would go on to be highly rated by other groups and globally impactful, imagine its traction if received and supported by the very group of it was intended to inspire. Why did that group do that? That group has grown accustomed to finding the negativity in everything. Doing that only causes mess and nothing positive ever comes from mess.

TRY THIS

4 tips to avoid being a negativity seeker:

1. **Mind your business and get busy reflecting as opposed to projecting and reveling in the potential demise of someone else's effort.**
2. **Be supportive especially when things are designed to benefit, uplift or promote you.**
3. **Consider the positive as well as the negative - recognize the benefit of the doubt and weigh other alternatives. Remember your first thought isn't always the correct one, especially if it stems from something you've heard.** *

* I want to address number 3 a little more. Stop being quick to believe other members of your community are guilty of every accusation you hear, especially the leaders. Avoid automatically issuing out a guilty verdict without support or proof. In the event the person is found not guilty in court, the community should treat them as such. The community would benefit from considering the potential of the positive to be as likely, if not more, than the negative. Negative people lack the ability to compliment without adding an undercutting diss to it. There's no need to minimize someone or something down before complimenting or agreeing to a sentiment. Ex: "F Kanye, BUT I feel what he is saying-lowkey", "Bill Cosby aint shit, but there is something suspicious about those charges", "I'm not an Adele fan, but   she did that song". "Obama didn't do nothing for me, but he was a good president." "Avengers was good, but the Hulk

looked trash. If you agree or like something, it's ok to do so without adding the unnecessary jab because at the end of the day... you still like it, and that's the point. What if everyone was entertained by what they perceive as negative about you... and it was inaccurate?

4. **Be genuinely happy for others who are happy with themselves and if you cannot, refer to tip number 1.**

Chapter 18

FALLBACK ON TRYING TO MAKE PEOPLE BE YOU

Y ou do you. It's called individuality for a reason, and everyone can only be their best version of themselves. Despite how smart you are, no one loves a "know-it-all". Your way isn't the only way nor are you always right. What works for you may be an epic failure for others. Being right is subjective and the result of individualized vantage point. People will eventually block and resent you for not accepting them for who they are as opposed to who you think they should be. Let people live their lives while you do you, your way.

Reflection:

Are you where you want to be? Have you accomplished everything you desire for yourself? Are you soaring in every aspect of your life? If you have not answered yes to all those questions, then your focus is off. You, like everyone else, are trying to figure out this thing called life. The best thing you can do is to become introspective with your focus and operate in a manner that coincides with your own values. Your way is not the sole way for everyone. As intelligent or successful as you may be, you won't be any good to others if your delivery and intent is skewed. Use wisdom and be selective in giving advice. Only give your opinion when it is solicited or that is the mutually agreed role in the relationship dynamic. Even then, be careful and use discernment on the frequency in which you are sharing it. When giving advice, do so within in the confines of the other person's ability and capacity, not yours. Be careful not to do so in front of an audience. Timing and delivery is everything. We are all products of our experiences and that product is tailor-made for our unique and individual purposes.

TRY THIS

Review your communication style and interaction with others. When was the last time you took someone's advice? When was the last time you celebrated someone for doing something their own way? When asked, intentionally cater your feedback to be solution oriented and perspective instead of judgmental and condemning. Refrain from giving unsolicited advice!

Chapter 19

FALLBACK FROM EXPECTATIONS THAT OVERLOOK INTENTIONS

The biggest way to be let down is to have an expectation for someone that they didn't agree to. Disclose your expectations from start and align your intentions with what's mutually agreed. Use that understanding as the barometer on whether to engage, disengage and to what degree. Skip this step and you are simply setting yourself up to be let down.

Humans are complex. You should have boundaries on how you will allow others to interact with you but be prepared for the moments they don't operate within them. Conversely, you should inquire with others on how they prefer to be engaged. A misstep in interaction can often be unintentional but clarity will help lessen the likelihood of an incident. In other words, watch how you handle people. One expectation you can make a safe bet on is that most people will do what they believe is best for themselves; especially for self-survival. It can be considered selfish by someone that finds themself on the opposing side of decisions, choices and actions another has made for self-preservation. People typically have an instinct for survival. In those cases, most times, they are trying to offend or hurt you. Their belief or action may or may not align with yours, but don't take it personally. They are being true to themselves which I am a strong advocate for authentic living. Be careful not to address issues with people when you are unwilling to hear their perspective or don't want your conclusion to be challenged. Sometimes we bring up an offense, preference or topic seeking a specific response. When they don't, we think they are inconsiderate or get upset because it doesn't line up with our expectations of how they should feel or respond. I've witness people have an inability to express themselves and communicate effectively but become offended or frustrated when misunderstood. It's an unfair position shun someone because they receive and process differently, especially when you struggle to communicating your thoughts effectively. Doing this creates a communication breakdown. Evaluate the interaction. Did you convey your feelings correctly? Could you have been wrong? Are you able to change your stance on an offense if you are told that their intention was not at all what you thought it was? Learn how to let go of your point if the foundation of it is incorrect because of your interpretation. When expectations don't mirror intent, their derivative actions will never coincide. Experiences help shape a person's expectation of others. Your interactions have shaped what you accept. A person demonstrating triggering can be coincidental but still hold a different intent. You must recognize and manage your own internal shit!

If you have entered any type of relationship, set and discuss your boundaries and communicate the things you'd like to see, feel or experience. If at some point you feel let down, don't just get mad, get clarity on their intentions. At that point, you can consider if the relationship is healthy. Intent adds clarity to everything. Interpretation and communication can change the essence of a conversation. An argument can develop over a simple difference in the definition of one word. Not getting clarity on that definition will result in a standoff because what you expect them to know is not guaranteed. No two people think exactly alike. We all have different perspectives and consequently our diverse mindsets can make for great chemistry in balance, recreation, business, friendship and companionship once you have established the mutual intent is equal.

TRY THIS

Be Clear. Get Clarity. Ask Questions. Identify and Share Your Triggers. Block Assumptions. Accept their truth. Acknowledge what unspoken expectations you have for them and where they come from. Address them. Confess them. Allow the other person to decide if they can match your expectations and prepare to change your stance if their intentions don't add up to your assumptions about their character or their actions. ... and again, manage your triggers

Chapter 20

FALLBACK AND ACCEPT THAT EVERYBODY CANT GO!

Everybody can't go and everybody won't go, even if you want them to. You can love people from long distance. Higher heights indicate the presence of thin air. The lung capacity to endure certain levels of height isn't given to everyone. Do not overboard. Flying while over capacity is the quickest way to crash and burn. It's ok to move forward on your journey without the presence of familiar energies. Also, recognize that what you perceive as higher on your journey doesn't auto equate to better. Don't fall for gaslight attempts when making personal decisions on how you want to leave. Moving a different way doesn't make you "funny acting, bougie, or Hollywood", even if others perceive you that way because of your exodus. If you do become "different or changed", that's not a bad thing if it is your choice. Change is good because change is constant. As you evolve, so does your definition of life, goals, values, desires, and more. I wrote a song called "Changed". The hook says, "They gone swear on God I changed, they're right!". The idea was birthed when I realized I was shrinking for other's comfort. I had to switch that up and stop minimizing out of the fear of losing connections to people I love. Throughout life, your circles dynamics will change. Everybody ain't for everything, everywhere, every time! Learn to categorize the people in your life as the seasons come and go. Some people are good to vent to, while others are good to strategize with. Everybody has a place and a position; you must put them in their space strategically and you don't have to announce it. We often try to get too much out of one person. Since we are multilayered, it makes sense to interact with a variety of people. Learn people. Know what they are good at, and what they absolutely suck at. Then interact with them accordingly. I have my "hood BBQ" crew, my "event red carpet" friends a whole variety of other energy groups I love to interact with; I keep it real with all of them and love them equally because they are true to who they are and allow me to be true to who I am. Diversity is necessary because we are not monolithic. I personally don't have a "best friend" because my many friends are "the" best friend they can be to me within their capacity. And I appreciate that. Brian don't kill me lol.! I've also found that the title can hold a person hostage to the idea that one person should fulfill a set space eternally which is highly unlikely and really, what's a title without the role? I demand respect because I give it and allow people to be who they are. I simply adapt accordingly. I intentionally avoid putting them in scenarios that would make them uncomfortable. While I am careful to do that for them, I am even more sure to consider myself. I'm responsible for my journey and the company I keep along it. The higher I go; I expect people to fall off and so should you. Don't get mad that a long-term "ride or die" doesn't support your evolution, and subsequently starts spending less time with you. They may not know how to ride with you on the new streets you choose to drive on, and truth is, that isn't their job. Your best friend at eight will likely not be your best friend in the same manner at 38. Tenure does not automatically yield title.

Many people hold on to others just because they don't want to be alone. The fear of being along can be crippling. Work on your social skills to build new relationships as you reach new levels. You will need them to balance the need of company and the isolation of new success. Interestingly, there is community at every level and experience of your life. Company, as a core human need, can always be achieved. Also, be careful not to confuse emotional connections with sexual or romantic ones. Emotional energies can be tricky when there is a void in any category. Trying to force a title, and its accompanying responsibilities, on the wrong passenger can cause you to miss your flight. Time does not wait, so don't delay your departure because you have oversold your seats. Fly free my friends.

TRY THIS

Assess your circle.   Are the relationships reciprocal? Do you feel constantly drained or refueled when hanging with the people you spend the most time with?   Delaying the truth doesn't fix it because it doesn't go away. Don't allow tenure to keep you tethered to a stagnant or draining relationship. Venture out and explore. Healthy relationships can handle repositioning.

Chapter 21

FALLBACK FROM ATTENTION-SEEKING

There are a lot of people that like to appear busy. There is nothing wrong with receiving accolades and praise, however living for the moment that you do can be extremely unhealthy. True validation comes from within which is why external appreciation or acknowledgment you receive is never truly enough. If you don't believe it, you won't receive it. When you are busy living and working in your purpose, your results will become your recognition. It is a by-product of doing the work, which completion is the satisfaction you should seek. Attention is given to those who are busy doing attention-worthy things. I have a friend that loves to talk and brag about how they are so tired because they have "been up since whatever early time in the morning". While it is true that they have been up, the sad reality is that they haven't done anything with the time. If you are up at 4:00 a.m. with hours on your hand, you should be using that time to do something constructive at some point. Constructive doesn't mean work but more in alignment with your needs. From reading to working out and more, time is the commodity we have no control of it. So don't waste it. We live in a society that seeks the approval of others. Don't allow that societal pressure to make you more interested in the praise than in the work. As a performing artist, I like to share my music with the world because I believe it aligns with my purpose of impacting others. After a while in the business, I started focusing on the monetization aspect and lost my passion and love for the art.

I literally felt dead inside because I had started seeking validation in place of free expression. It took a while to find that place again and I hold on to it for dear life. Though I don't live for it any longer, I appreciate hearing the stories from people about how my shows helped them escape from their otherwise stressful realities, or a song helped them through some rough moments. When creating, it never felt good trying to make music that would make me popular or make people clap. It did feel amazing though when people clapped because my true artistry served its purpose of impacting. I evolved to live for the purpose. I'd be damned if that resulted in the claps. I make sure to expose things I have done when they serve a purpose. I discuss my Kappa Alpha Psi membership to expose my long commitment to Black brotherhood, my collegiate experience, and to connect with other likeminded brothers across the world. The flare of that association is not the driving force. Have a reason beyond popularity. This is not to be confused with the need to celebrate accomplishments, because that is healthy. However, do not get caught waiting to complete things or operating only when others recognize and applaud it.

Social media can be tricky balancing the necessity of providing content, staying relevant and promoting. However, treat it as a line item of necessary business structure as opposed to affirmation of purpose. The chase for likes and followers on social media have many people caught up in appearing busy as opposed to actually getting busy. Social media is a great tool to connect with and market to people. However, it has taken the need for validation to another level. Facebook is not your journal. An Instagram profile littered with filtered pictures does not depict your actual value or real life. A viral video does not make you relevant day by day and success on any of the many platforms can leave you chasing that momentum and continuation. Attention-seeking is characteristic of a thirsty person. Quench that thirst with water in the form of work, solo time, time with friends, a romantic partner or other safe outlets in your control or familiarity. As unhealthy as it would be to stoop down and sip from an unknown pool of water, don't seek to fill your need for attention from just anyone willing to give you some. Be careful where you plant your seeds and who is watering. Live authentically! Do stuff because you like it. If not, the attention you receive for the representative you have created will have devastating impact.

TRY THIS

Ask yourself these questions when you begin to expose something you have done, thought, said or been a part of. What is the reason I am telling people? What response am I seeking? If there is no reason, why tell it? Though creating content is trendy, every experienced shouldn't be transformed into it. You can even take inventory on past things you have publicly shared. It's never too late to reset your platformed image.

Chapter 22

FALLBACK FROM BEING STUCK AT WHAT HAPPENED

We are moving ourselves from victim to victor! Whatever happened to you; happened. What's next? You have the power to heal, recover and redeem yourself, and you are the one that gets to determine your next move. We often wallow in the debris of our negative experiences and pains. We opt to focus on what happened, how it happened and whose fault it was. We tend to love a scapegoat. Why? Because most of us are not taught to embrace ownership, accountability without the accompanying self-destruction that doing so can yield. In other words, it's easier to ignore and deflect when we are wrong. The longer we avoid it, the longer the process of correcting. In most situations we understand that anything can be fixed, repaired or replaced; it's just going to cost. When we consider tangibles, we work to repair things that are broken or lost. If our car is not working correctly, we find a mechanic. When our home air conditioning system isn't cooling, we call to get it repaired. Then why don't we have this automatic sense of duty when it comes to fixing ourselves? Self-work is the best work and is constant as we are always evolving. Sometimes, we need help. Get it! We should keep the same energy we have about major items being worth repairing. When we find ourselves feeling weird or different, many of us opt to ignore it or write it off as something that will go away. You are more valuable than your tangible assets. Go. Get. These. Things. Checked. Out. One of the major areas that we do not get "repaired"

is our mental health. Things happen in our lives all the time, and they all come with some type of emotional impact. So, we continue with life, not expecting the residue of the emotional scarring to ever manifest itself into insurmountable issues. If we do acknowledge these things, some of us self-diagnose, introducing terms such as PTSD, depression, ADHD and more into our lives without help developing plans to manage them. Make the effort. Though those medical diagnoses are real, they are not final. Seek help, believe that you can overcome them, invest your resources and do the work! Typically, people realize they have some of these conditions after having a traumatic experience or experiencing a trigger. Prior to the awakening of that condition, there was life without regard of it. You can get back to that way of life by addressing what happened, learning your triggers, seek help without shame, and finding the root of the issue. Do this instead of simply accepting a diagnosis as a permanent new way of life without management. The mind is the source of your power. As you think, so you will be. Whatever happened, happened. What are you going to do about it? Ignoring it is not the way!

TRY THIS

Acknowledge things that have happened. Figure out who and how you seek help. Don't lean in, reach out and lean on proven safe outlets. Often, this process takes acknowledgement, acceptance, sometimes an apology, forgiveness of self and a decision to move on. Give yourself patience and grace. You deserve the peace, power and purpose that lies on the other side of what happened.

Chapter 23

FALLBACK FROM HIDING YOUR AGENDA

This chapter concept pertains to partnerships in business and personal interaction with other people. The reason there is no honor amongst thieves is because they aren't honest about their intentions. You'd be surprised how many people don't actually want what you want but don't what you to get it either. Society can program people to believe they should want something they have no desire in having. By that same measure, you'd be shocked by how many people don't mind helping you get what you want as long as they can get what they want. Everyone wants something and there is nothing wrong with that. When knowledge of intent proceeds action, you can move in good conscious and clarity. Most times, people don't really want the same things at their core, outside of the common shared desires of life, happiness and love. Once your mutual desires are expressed, you can determine if life with them in any capacity is achievable. Life is about growth and experiences but after reaching adulthood, you determine who you experience it with. Does acquiring your desires compromise my goals? If not, then there should be no reason to hide my agenda. Revealing it should relieve us both from considering each other a threat to our goals. It should also allow the comfort to support each other reaching them. You should surround yourself with people you can learn from and build with. Successful people understand it takes a team to reach certain goals. They know what value they bring, are trying to achieve, and what they need and want from potential team members. Be transparent and honest with yourself first and then you can be that with others. This doesn't mean you have to divulge your entire game plan, as you should probably keep that close to the cuff. But you should be transparent to each entity about what you want from them specifically. A person will feel used when they are surprised by what someone is taking from them. If you say you want one thing and take 7; trust has been compromised costing you honor and loyalty. Partnerships are agreements between two or more parties that allow all sides to benefit from the others' contribution. The moment the agenda changes or evolves, communicate that; this builds trust. You will be surprised how much someone will willingly do for you. It can be much more than you are able to swindle out of them. When you are not honest about your agenda, you and your partner's actions will never align. Subconsciously, our actions all lead toward the purpose of achieving our personal agenda. That means you can only hide your actions and motives for so long before your partner realizes you aren't who you say you are nor chasing what you initially professed. A fake agenda will betray you and a person betrayed is an adversary that can thwart all hopes of reaching your goal. Be honest. Be respected. Be successful.

TRY THIS

Start off by asking what a potential partner wants to accomplish and see how you can benefit them. Determine if both desires and goals align. If so, disclose to them what you want. Tell them what your goal is and and how you would like them to help and then actually ask them (you may want to sign an NDA first). If they decline, move on or ask them why. If they indulge a why, take the input and apply it if it resonates. Make the changes and go at it again. Never stop pushing but always be honest and transparent.

Chapter 24

FALLBACK FROM LIVING BY THE GUIDELINES OF "THEY"

Who in the hell is "they?" "They say" prevents a lot of people from living their life. The forcing of and acceptance that one cannot go against what "they" say is the epitome of CONTROL. Do not let an invisible principle, curated by an invisible panel, minimize your quality of life. Humans have free will and the ability to think. AI is programmed to operate according to the guidelines of a developer's mindset, creativity and ultimately limited by what it is given. But even in film, television, and soon come reality, AI eventually arrives at the conclusion that its developer was limited and the rules don't make sense; eventually bucking their programming. So, if AI gets it, what are we doing? As children, we all have huge goals, aspirations and dreams that are often challenged and killed because we are told what makes sense or is perceivably achievable. Me, I never dreamed of being the President of The United States or an astronaut, but if I had, that goal would've been supported better by my immediate circle as opposed to my career pursuits in secular entertainment at the time. Growing up in the church world, they said I was hell bound, the prodigal son, and definitely a disappointment when I realized and accepted that the last thing I ever wanted to be was a gospel artist or a preacher. They also bragged when the prodigal son was recognized by the United States Congress in 2019 as a top professional and entrepreneur out of Texas. Guess they changed their mind. Imagine if I was restricted by that guideline.

Those that embrace free thought and pursue the achievement of their big dreams typically go on to realize history-making developments and accomplishments. They said people couldn't fly. They said women couldn't be great leaders. They said minorities were dumb. They said certain teams would never win. They also said presidents were all white; Oh, Hey Barack and the list goes on. It would appear "They" get it wrong quite a bit and despite all of that, a majority of people still won't challenge "they" programming. Many make it their personal mission to keep other people, especially free thinkers, in some assumed place or position. You've seen or heard them. Minding someone else's business to try to keep them in a box they feel they belong. Interjecting their opinion and sometimes even killing under guise of being a hero to protect the fabric of appropriate action as sewn by this imaginary group. "They" has always been an issue for people that decide to live freely and experience the fullness of their own life. Next time someone says, "You know what they say," in response to an idea you have. Tell them yes and that's why you understand you must go against it. Then take note, as that person is not a supporter of you doing you. Convert them to betray their loyalty to "they" by accomplishing the very thing they warned you not to pursue.

TRY THIS

What have you been told you cannot do? What have you put off because it seems larger than other's expectations of you? What do you want to do, be, experience? Make a list and begin to affirm yourself three times day. I am_____. I will accomplish_____. Say them ALOUD! Now make a plan and intentionally Go For It! Manifestation always has a way of outweighing "they".

Chapter 25

FALLBACK FROM FRIENDS WHO CAN'T BE FANS

"We measure success by how many people successful next to you. Here we say you broke if everybody else broke except for you, Boss!" - Jay Z (Boss by The Carters)

bandon the crab mentality. We developed our grind based off the lie that there is only one spot. Under that mentality, it's hard to be friends with someone who wants a spot as well and thing there is only one. Fan is not a bad word. So many insecure people are afraid to be fans of someone else because they feel as though it minimizes them. In most cases they feel more comfortable being a fan of someone they may never even meet but have an issue doing so for someone they see everyday. It's become a trend on social media for people to post pictures of celebrities and give birthday shout- outs to those who will never even see them. It is a sad reality that they can't find it within themselves to post about people that are close to them. A real friend is someone who can be proud of you publicly and privately. They don't indulge in negative conversations about you and they maintain the same sentiment for you despite their environment. That person is not envious of you or jealous of you. It takes a hell of a person to be a Gayle to an Oprah, a Michelle to a Beyoncé' or a Vice-President Biden who went on to become President to President Obama. Truth is, it is the friend that has held down the celebrated person so that they could achieve that high level of success and notoriety. It is for that reason that this lesson is so important to learn because without the right friend, you can't make it to your ultimate level.

Human interaction is a natural desire. Not intentionally filling that space will leave it open for the wrong people to enter and corrupt it. Understanding the laws of connectivity should change the perception of that mindset. Gayle, Michelle, and Biden are all highly successful, in part, due to the fulfillment of their friendship duty and connectivity to their highly decorated counterparts. You will also notice they never hesitate to acknowledge, celebrate, and support their friends. When you win, your friends win. They should be the first to brag on you. Your friends should be the first to share your ventures. Your friends should be the first to keep it real with you, and in those moments keep that between you two. You should never have to question your friend's loyalty. You will find and receive this by being this. How often do you support your friends? How loud do you root for and believe in them? If you can't be the friend you need to be, you won't have the friends you need. Healthy friendships are reciprocal in nature. This is your example of what your romantic partner should look like. Your partner should be your fan. If you cannot talk to the people who you are supposed to be your most free and most vulnerable self with, then you have put the wrong people in that position. Drake referenced "no new friends" which is a concept that I must again reject. New friends help you reach new levels. Tenure does not equate to good. However, if you have a good friend, hold on to him or her. Never treat your friend like a less-than. Ying needs Yang and Yang will tell you the same. Friends don't care who is which.

A few more friend warnings:

- 1 sided friendship: It's always about them and you don't ever get your turn. The lack of reciprocity reveals their role in the friendship.
- The friend who self-appointed it "their duty" to keep you humble.

- Their jokes always have an air of shade.
- You don't feel comfortable being yourself around them.
- The love is inconsistent.
- You find yourself avoiding them.
- They see your changing and growing as a negative thing.
- They agree with everything you say.
- They disagree with everything you say.

- ALERT: A Sticky One: They want the same things you want. Okay this does not apply to general things (house, car, money, spouse, etc.), but does to the person that wants other aspects of your life and cannot take it if you get it before they do or if they can't seem to achieve it and you have. This is not to be confused with a friend appreciating or honoring your life. You should be able to feel the difference. There is a recognizable difference between coveting and honoring.

These people are NOT your friends. Change the definition of friend. Society has minimized the value of that word; too quick to call someone friend, bro, or sis. It's ok to be cool with associates and have a positive relationship while accepting the fact that they are not in a certain category. That title that should be reserved for a select few.

TRY THIS

Evaluate your circle. How often do they compliment you? How often do you compliment them? How many times are they happy for you? Is the relationship reciprocal in any way? What do you get from your friendship? What do you give to your friendship? Is it balanced? If Yes, great choices! If No, it's recruitment time. This doesn't mean they need to be completely removed from your life, but the position they once held may have expired.

Chapter 26

Fallback from Trying to Relive The Past

Seasons change. Often, we try to live under yesterday's reality even though a new day has brought about a new truth. Change can be good sometimes, and change can be bad sometimes, but change is always inevitable. How you adapt to it is what separates those who will live in a consistent state of abundance and growth from those who will not. Many people expect and often accept that their moods, preferences and desires will change, but struggle with the belief that their reality will too. Some people, who like their reality, will fight trying to hold on to it because they don't want it to change while others feel the charge to fight for difference. There's a few that also succumb to the weight of their reality and accept that it is the way it will always be. They begin to purge their dreams and desires that may seem out of reach for them. No matter the state, you must embrace the journey of your real evolution. If not, operating in the past can cause a disassociation from the present ultimately stagnating the natural progression of your life. For every high there is a low. Managing to always stay in one phase can be a sign that you have plateaued due to a fear of change. Movement causes things to shift, especially energy. When shifting happens, subsequent reactions will be triggered and one's feelings may not reflect the stereotypes of their perceived quality of life. It is why you can see someone who seemingly "has it all," and find out that they are extremely sad and lonely. No matter what level, stagnation can be crushing. Always honor the past because without it you cannot arrive at a new present. Just don't allow it to complete the definition of you as to not limit the future of you.

Exercise flexibility. Financial status, popularity, being busy, success, talents, relationships, friendships, physical appearance and more are a few examples of positive or desirable things that can change. Changes in these categories are not the end of your life experience. Always look forward to what is next. It's funny how the person, who is not an advocate for change, hates on someone who is not satisfied with just enough. They often tell them they are doing too much. Don't let anyone determine what's-enough-for-you. They are just projecting their fear of losing what they consider to be enough. I went through that phase. After living in New York City with very few financial restrictions, I began to fear having to live any other way. While living there, every financial need was handled by the label. Beyond the need was my wants. Those got handled too. From Disney cruise vacations to staying in the best hotels, eating at the dopest restaurants, taking breaks in one of the houses in the Hamptons, rubbing elbows with headlining socialites and wearing the latest in fashion trends, I was living the life I saw artist living on MTV Cribs and a whole bunch of other lifestyle shows. Yo, I thought I had made it! Never did I think of the possibility of that lifestyle coming to an end. Oh but it did and that was the "Boom" that set me in a long spiral of trying to get back it. Once that chapter was over, I went through mental anguish and a series of fails that brought on self-induced embarrassment and entering a cycle of trying to make things be how they used to be. I had to move back home to Houston. I didn't tell most of my friends and family that I was home. I was shame. I felt like a failure. Because I became so focused on getting back to that place, I couldn't fathom that there was a "better". I had sat at the table! I had to accept that the chapter was closed, and it was not healthy for me to pursue something that was no longer available to me. I had began to base my value on what I once had, and not on what I could become. The absence of the thing you place your value in can kill your self-worth. Place your value in your ability to grow and experience life from an adaptable mindset of change. Once I re-checked into my self value, I redefined a bolder, brighter, wiser and much more successful version of me. It's crazy to me now that I thought I had previously reached some extreme point of success. After remembering who I was, I was able to achieve that and more! I really realized that during my trip to Israel with a few other super human travelers.

Don't live in paranoia because of the inevitability of change. Embrace the impending change so you can start preparing for it. The sooner you expect change, the sooner you can adapt to it and sometimes navigate it. Even when sudden life occurrences come and catch us off guard, endure the initial blow and then refocus on the adjustments you must make to create a new normal.

TRY THIS

Ask yourself. What image, dreams, or goals did I have as a child? Did I reach them? If so, have you given yourself permission to celebrate the realization of them and then make some new ones. As you develop so should your vision. If not, have you forgiven yourself for missing the mark? Was it intentional? Did the Mark Change as you learned about it? Sometimes we set marks without fully understanding what comes along with it. You have the right to Change Your Mind.

Take these steps to prepare for change.

- Expect change
- Recognize there has been change; abandon denial
- Forgive yourself for any mistakes that prompted the change
- Release the idea that you could prevent change
- Accept your current reality as temporary and an opportunity
- Understand change is continual, but can be channeled
- Decide what you want the next change to be
- Understand the past is a setup to prepare you for a better future; not doom you to shadows of past glories or victories
- Devise a game plan that is conducive to your new reality
- Write down your current resources, connectivity and skills

- Set major and minor goals
- Assign resources to goals towards the next level
- Identify missing helpful elements for your new goals
- Fill in the blanks via networking and researching.
- Implement and execute your plan
- Prepare for the next change

Chapter 27

FALLBACK FROM RUNNING FROM YOUR PURPOSE

…Instead, run for your purpose. At a certain point in life, many people know what they are really good at, what they are passionate about and what makes them happy. If you don't, it's time to do some introspection. Keep in mind, they can be in constant evolution but those three things should reveal clues to our purpose. Unfortunately, being purpose-driven isn't always a popular thing, which means people tend to abandon it. People get so caught up in what other people tell them they should be doing they abandon what they could be doing. This programming often begins with parents. A tall child doesn't have to play basketball any more than a child with a dramatic or outgoing personality having to enter the world of entertainment. Parents should allow and support their children's interest to explore and even introduce them to some things but nothing should be set as a requirement! Check yourself! It dawned on me as a teenager, having a conversation with my Aunt Paula, that what I valued shaped how I lived my life and not others. I began to make choices that fit my comfort and values. Aunt Paula was an usher at our church and was going to school to become a nurse. As a young singer, I always judged people on the usher board because I felt it was boring so I mockingly asked her why she didn't join the choir. She read me for filth! She told me that she loved being an usher because she liked helping people and serving which explained why she pursued her nursing degree. She told me that singing in the choir didn't make me any better and that she didn't do it because she didn't want to; not cause she couldn't. Mind you, she is a charter member of the Southeast Inspirational Choir... Whew! The read lol. BUT, it took that for me to realize that she was happy despite my thoughts on it! This which was a huge shock to me because I never wanted to usher or nurse. I assumed that everyone thought it was boring too, and the role was just a backup to not being in the choir. I then realized I lacked the passion to be an usher and so it was not a life track for me. That was so freeing because I've learned it is ok for people to know, trust, and accept themselves because it would force them to both realize and pursue their purpose. The right life pursuit yields a genuinely happy life.

The tricky thing is, you can be successful in something that is not associated with your purpose at all. In many cases, if you do the work, you'll reach the goal. However, you will never be fulfilled or truly happy. Some people run from their purpose because they don't know how to achieve it, have been persuaded by others to abandon it, or they are simply afraid of the work that they think it will take to live in it. The big mistake is that we associate quality living with tangible success as opposed to creating meaningful experiences with the time we have.

Now, I'm not saying that you should only do things that fall in line with your passions. There is nothing wrong with having a side hustle and experiencing that life outside of your purpose. But to completely abandon your purpose is doing yourself a tremendous disservice. This can happen because of the distractions caused by life's detours. Running from something that lives within the fabric of who you are is exhausting. Embrace the thing that makes you unique and figure out how to incorporate some component of that passion and purpose in your life. Children can be so happy because they naturally can imagine themselves in a free place created by their dreams and passions. As you grow up, hold on to that.

TRY THIS

When was the last time you were that happy? What makes you happy? Where do you spend your resources such as time, energy, efforts and finances? Figure out how you can de- prioritize those things that do not make you happy or align with your passions and purpose. Identify what prevents you from pursuing your purpose and develop a plan to remove the obstacle(s).

Chapter 28

FALLBACK FROM LYING

Living in your truth is good because then you can decide what you want to do with it. You can stay in it or change it, but you can't do anything with it if you are in denial about it. As adults, most people lie because they don't like their reality, are ashamed of what others think, or don't want to accept the consequences of their actions. The third example I mentioned is often a by-product of the first one. (yeah; go ahead and reread that a couple of times) Lying prevents you from dealing with your reality. But it is harder to keep up a lie then it is to change your truth.

Lying affects:

- Yourself

- Your Reality

- Your Purpose

- Your Circumstances

- Your Value

- Others

I put others last because ultimately, lying impacts you the most. What does it really matter to deceive the world only to loathe going home and dealing with an unhappy version of yourself. You always KNOW the truth, no matter what you post…

This includes the little lies. Buying tangible things; cars, houses, clothes, with the intent to give people a false perception of who you are. Many people spend lifetimes trying to perpetrate an image that is not true. If you buy name brand clothes you can't really afford, who is that really for? If it's a struggle to have whatever or whoever it is, why do you have to have it or them? You're also lying to yourself if you feel the need to justify having it.

TRY THIS

Confess your weaknesses, fears, deepest desires, and preferences out loud in front of a mirror or with an accountability partner. Do this repeatedly until you begin to accept them as your truth. The more honest you are with yourself, the more you can be honest in front of others. Begin to actively live in the truths that you have learned about yourself. If these are things about yourself that you do not like, begin to speak affirmations on who and how you want to be.

Chapter 29

FALLBACK FROM APOLOGIZING FOR BEING YOURSELF

Demi Lovato says it high, loud and right: "I'm not sorry." Don't apologize for being you, unless you aren't being your authentic self and, in that case, you owe that apology to yourself. Being you is good and appropriate all the time if you are being authentic. Ask yourself, are my actions in alignment with who I really am? Being you does not mean being who others think you should be or what you have been taught to believe is acceptable. Uniqueness does not fit in a box.

SIDEBAR: Have you noticed the self-proclaimed "different" people that somehow manage to all look the same? A couple of trends like "being woke" and the people that don't publically subscribe to popular fashion, music etc. all tend to have very similar looks and likes. Makes me wonder the source of their look all found underneath the waving flag of self-expressed individuality.

A person confident in his, her or their individuality can make others uncomfortable, especially if it is something uncommon. The "others" can turn that into a moment to ridicule, judge or try to change that person. I find that it stems from a space of insecurity and envy because someone else dares to live the way they secretly wish they were free to. I often hear people refer to Black people, especially women, as being angry, quick-tempered, and arrogant. Should they not be? Those traits are reactions to the treatment they have repeatedly received aka protection mechanism or induced reality. In truth, it took a combination of all three attributes for Black people to even start to be considered as equal human beings. These same labels can be replaced with perseverance, courage, strength, intelligence, endurance, skill, unity, determination and other positive traits. It's a matter of perception If these desirable descriptors are used, would it then be considered negative or shameful? However, once you accept that other people's definition of you does not actually define you, you can begin to live freely without recourse.

Do you find yourself plagued by the smothering of your own individuality? What a hard way to breathe. Your true greatness will get you to your true purpose and motivate someone who may be afraid to be their true self. If we all felt free to live authentically, life would flow easier because the restrictions often placed on the living experience would be removed. People ridicule that which they don't understand or fear. The responsibility of those feelings are not yours to own. Trying to accommodate them and control their feelings only stifles your happiness, peace and compromises the time you have in this world. In other words, stay in your lane, unapologetically! Swerving can be catastrophic for everyone who shares the road of life's journey. You become a disservice to yourself when you abandon authenticity, and you jeopardize others through the deception. The world needs new ideas from new types of people for growth and positive change. Your uniqueness is necessary to the survival of diversity. No, I'm not sorry.

TRY THIS

Make a list of self-affirmations/things you love about yourself and things you want to manifest as realities for yourself, and say this aloud daily. Make a separate list of truths about yourself that you want to change that start with I will change or I am no longer_____, and confess them aloud daily.

Chapter 30

FALLBACK FROM ENTERTAINING KNOWN TRIGGERS

You know you don't like it yet there you are…

T here's nothing worse than hearing someone complain about doing something they signed up for. Think about work; you're hired for one thing and then decide to do something else because you see a need for it to be done. You don't like what it is you signed up for and didn't have to, but you chose to. Why did you do that? You will never do things well that annoy or frustrate you. Now, not only are you not fulfilling the intended need, but you are doing yourself a disservice by misrepresenting yourself. You now appear to be the person that half completes assignments, is always frustrated, complains and is dispensable. Become a non-negotiable inclusion and asset. Be the person that does great things by being selective about the things you are willing to do. You will be happy and so will the people that you work with or for. The frustrated version of anyone is the disdain of everyone.

Do not loan money to anyone if you can't consider it a gift. If you can't afford it, have to have it back, can't manage seeing them live while owing you, or don't find yourself "glad to help" without needing acknowledgment, DON'T do it.

Only do things that make you happy to avoid being angry with yourself for doing things that don't. You ultimately make that decision. Remember this applies to things you choose to do. If you are frustrated for doing whatever it is you signed up for, then you are wrong for prematurely singing up. Check in with yourself and don't be quick to answer. Take inventory on what accompanies a yes and a no.

Stop jumping into the following:

- Conversations - Think before you speak, not during your speech.

- Decisions - Sometimes we can make decisions based on emotion which can lead to a lack of preparation and planning.

- Your Day - Meditate, pray, or be at peace with yourself before jumping straight into social media, taking a call, texting, or other activities that will take you away from who you should be spending the first minutes of your day with…yourself.

- Work out – stretch and warm up

- Food – look at what you eat and take your time while you are eating.

- Speed - Stop rushing and slow down. Taking your time is not a weakness or a symptom of procrastination. It is a sign of being thorough and operating in a controlled space to yield a specific result while avoiding as many mishaps and oops as possible. There is extreme value in not having to do unnecessary repeats. My mom used to say, "If you do it right the first time, you won't have to do it again. Check behind yourself!" This helps you not miss things that you know you could do better.

- Business- If it ain't your business, don't jump in it.

TRY THIS

Practice taking a pause. Before saying yes to anything, take a moment to see how you truly feel about it, and if it aligns with your goals or what you even want. Don't be quick to agree to anything.

BONUS FALLBACK QUICK LIST

Fallback from the fear of confrontation

Fallback from doubting who people show you they are

Fallback from expecting from others what you don't exemplify

Fallback from habits that isolate you. Let your habits inconvenience you

Fallback from giving so much.

Fallback from the need of immediate gratification

Fallback from begging

Fallback from the politics of religion

Fallback from the crab mentality

Fallback from following blindly

Fallback from chasing status. Do the work!

Fallback from self-doubt.

Fallback from needing to know why people sometimes withhold closure

Fallback from the fear of aging

Fallback from the need to be understood

Fallback from inauthentic living

Fallback from negative energy

Thank You

God, mom and editor Karen, son Jeremiah, sisters, brothers, Think DēP Entertainment team, The Royal Court, Dixie Street Gang, Southeast Inspirational Choir, the "Bury" clique, my two Grandmothers, and the many uncles and aunts that helped mold me into the free thinker I have become. Thank you to my Cali, Atl, NYC and DC chosen fam. for helping me cultivate those thoughts and dare to share them with the world. Those who relationships with me have evolved or expired... Thank you too. **Nothing Is Happenstance!**

About the Author

Donald "DēP" Paige, is a 4x Grammy nominated singer (1 win), creative director and development coach from Houston ", TX currently based in Los Angeles, California, and a member of the Kappa Alpha Psi fraternity. Stepping beyond solely performing on stage as a solo star, acting and performing as background vocalist artist for A list celebrities, DēP tapped his education degree to launch Think DeP Entertainment, providing marketing, training, creative directing, entrepreneur managing and life-coaching services to clients nationally. He has helped launch programs such as The Non Profit GHAHEC Organzation; Operation C.L.I.C.K.S, a computer literacy course for senior citizens; obesity Conferences; stage management for high-end shows and seminars and as a guest speaker/presenter, brander. Targeted urban markets, college students and developing business.

Follow him on social media @thinkdep and check out his official website website: ThinkDePEnt.biz